John Camden Hotten

A garland of Christmas carols, ancient and modern

Including some never before given in any collection

John Camden Hotten

A garland of Christmas carols, ancient and modern
Including some never before given in any collection

ISBN/EAN: 9783741181634

Manufactured in Europe, USA, Canada, Australia, Japa

Cover: Foto ©Andreas Hilbeck / pixelio.de

Manufactured and distributed by brebook publishing software (www.brebook.com)

John Camden Hotten

A garland of Christmas carols, ancient and modern

A GARLAND OF CHRISTMAS CAROLS, ANCIENT AND MODERN.

INCLUDING SOME NEVER BEFORE GIVEN IN ANY COLLECTION.

EDITED, WITH NOTES,

BY JOSHUA SYLVESTER.

LONDON:
JOHN CAMDEN HOTTEN, PICCADILLY.
1861.

CONTENTS.

	Page
INTRODUCTION	ix

PART I.

LEGENDARY AND NARRATIVE CAROLS.

CAROL for St. Stephen's Day	1
The Virgin and Child	5
The Three Kings	9
The Golden Carol of Melchior, Balthazar, and Gaspar, the Three Kings of Cologne	13
For Christmas Day in the Morning	15
I saw Three Ships	18
The Carnal and the Crane	22
The Angel Gabriel from God	29
The Holy Well	32
All you that are to Mirth inclined	36
Gloria Tibi, Domine	41
The Cherry-tree Carol	44
Dives and Lazarus	50
The Moon shines bright	54
God rest you Merry Gentlemen	57
A Virgin most pure	61

vi CONTENTS.

	Page
The Worcestershire Carol	64
Come rejoice, all good Christians	67
The Seven Virgins	71
Last Night as I lay sleeping	74

PART II.

RELIGIOUS CAROLS.

"In Excelsis Gloria"	77
Welcome Yule	79
A Carol on the Birth of Christ	81
Carol, with Lullaby	84
New Prince, New Pomp	87
For Christmas Day	89
The Shepherds' Song	91
Christmas Tide	94
Hymn on the Nativity of my Saviour	95
The Angels' Song	97
Remember, O thou Man	99
A Christmas Carol	104
The Star Song	107
An Ode on the Birth of our Saviour	109
Christmas Day	111
The Virgin Mother	113
Joy to the World	117
Hark! the herald Angels sing	118
Whilst Shepherds watch'd	120
Hark! all around the Welkin rings	122
Mortals, awake, with Angels join	124
A New Christmas Carol	127
Christ was born on Christmas Day	129

CONTENTS.

Part III.
NUMERAL CAROLS.

	Page
The Seven Joys	132
A New Dial	136
Man's Duty; or, Meditation for the Twelve Hours of the Day	138

Part IV.
CAROLS IN PRAISE OF THE HOLLY AND IVY.

Holly and Ivy made a great Party	141
Here comes Holly	143
Nay, Ivy, nay	144
Holly Carol	146
The Holly and the Ivy	148

Part V.
CAROLS IN PRAISE OF THE BOAR'S HEAD.

Tidings I bring you for to tell	150
The Boar's Head in Hand I bring	152
The Boar's Head in Hand bring I	155
The Boar's Head that we bring here	157
The Boar is dead	159

Part VI.
FESTIVE CAROLS.

Anglo-Norman Carol	161
Sir Christmas	165
A Carol in praise of Ale	167

CONTENTS.

	Page
A Carol for a Wassail Bowl	170
God bless the Master of this House	174
Come bring with a Noise	175
The Wassail	177
Merry Christmas	180
All you that in this House be here	186
Cheer	189
Old Christmas returned	190
Now Thrice Welcome Christmas	196
Christmas Day approaches near	198
Christmas Customs	200
Christmas is a coming	202
The Wassailers' Carol	204
Wassailers' Carol	207
Carol for the Poor	209

INTRODUCTION.[1]

SOME years ago I walked down to Seven Oaks, in Kent, to enjoy the blessed Christmas. This village is one of a few in the vicinity of London uncontaminated by a railway with its crowd of giddy visitors from the great city.

I had just returned from abroad, after a long residence there, and even the minor observances and customs of the season possessed a pleasing novelty and charm. As I passed through Bromley I observed the shops, filled with viands for the great yearly feast, decorated with the emblems of the season.

---

[1] The above representation of a Wassail Bowl is from a carving on a chimney-piece of an old mansion formerly existing at Birling, Kent. The terms *Wassail* and *Drinkhail* are both from the Anglo-Saxon. The former is equivalent to the modern phrase, " Your health ; " and the latter means, in plain English, " Drink health." See under " Festive Carols," page 161.

INTRODUCTION.

The little cottage on the road-side had its sprigs of holly in the window, and ruddy children stood at the door with faces that betokened how near was the general holiday. As I drew towards my destination I occasionally passed a peasant carrying the, to him, sumptuous meal for the morrow,—perhaps the bountiful gift of the good lady at the manor-house—or bearing on his shoulder a block to light up his cottage hearth in honour of Christmas-tide. I could not help thinking, as I moved along, that on the eve of this glorious day all nature seemed to sink into repose after the labours and storms of the past year.

The quiet village of Seven Oaks exhibited that neat and cleanly aspect so often admired by visitors to this country when passing through our more orderly rural districts. The trimmed hedge-rows, whitened door-steps, and glistening window-panes, with the prim and happy old people passing about making preparations for the morrow, pictured forth a delightful scene of order and contentment.

Fatigued with my walk, I retired to rest early. A bright moon was shining into my chamber, and through the window I could see lights moving about the apartments of Knowle House,[2] a short distance

---

[2] The magnificent seat of the Earl Amherst, formerly the residence of the Sackvilles, Dukes of Dorset. The house covers upwards of five acres of ground, and furnishes specimens of the architecture of various ages.

across the park, indicating that the great people were also preparing for the mirthful time. I had not been in the room very long before my ears were saluted by a sweet music of youthful voices. Opening the casement I found some young villagers singing a Carol. The tune was plaintive, and simple in the extreme, and appeared to harmonize exactly with the scene and the occasion. It was the old Carol of "God rest you Merry Gentlemen," and if a critic should aver that the piece was more appropriate for the following day, I can only say that the melody sounded very delightful on that still and frosty night. After a time the little folks withdrew, and I heard their voices in the distance, apparently not far from a neighbouring farm house. As Irving remarked on a similar occasion, the notes of the Carolists as they receded became more soft and aërial, and seemed to accord with quiet and moonlight. I listened and listened; they became more and more tender and remote; and, as they gradually died away, my head sunk upon my pillow, and I fell asleep. In the early morning my window was again saluted by a joyous song, and going to it I discovered two young men and three girls " welcoming with sweet music the blessed morn."

Such is a brief narrative of Christmas associations that I always remember with pleasure. Although personal, I trust these reminiscences will be considered a not inappropriate introduction to our subject.

INTRODUCTION.

Christmas Carols doubtless had their origin in that celestial music which Milton describes in his "Hymn to the Nativity:"—

> "Such music (as 'tis said)
> Before was never made
> But when of old the sons of morning sung,
> While the Creator great
> His constellations set."

The oldest religious hymns, sung by the early Christians in the centuries immediately following Christ's death, have not been handed down to us. The most ancient Carols that we now possess date from the Middle Ages, and consist generally of portions of miracle plays, religious spectacles, and old religious legends.

Thus one miracle play, the most popular, perhaps, of any of these biblical representations, "The Creation of the World," has supplied several Carols. It was acted in London so late as the reign of Queen Anne. The introduction in the same performance of Adam and Eve, Herod, and the Duke of Marlborough, cannot be considered as good taste, however much the blending of antediluvian with current history may have contributed to fill Mr. Heatly's purse. The handbill to the performance reads thus ;—I have italicised those scenes which now form the subject of Carols :—

INTRODUCTION.

BY HER MAJESTIE'S PERMISSION.

AT HEATLY'S BOOTH,

Over against the Cross Daggers, next to Mr. Miller's Booth: During the time of Bartholomew fair, will be presented a little Opera, call'd *The Old Creation of the World*, newly reviv'd, with the addition of the Glorious Battle obtained over the French and Spaniards by his Grace the Duke of Marlborough.

THE CONTENTS ARE THESE.

1. The Creation of Adam and Eve.
2. The intreagues of Lucifer in the Garden of Eden.
3. Adam and Eve driven out of Paradise.
4. Cain going to plow, Abel driving sheep.
5. Cain killeth his brother Abel.
6. Abraham offering his son Isaac.
7. *Three Wisemen of the East guided by a Star, who worship him.*
8. *Joseph and Mary flee away by night upon an ass.*
9. *King Herod's cruelty, his men's spears laden with children.*
10. *Rich Dives invites his friends, and orders his porter to keep the beggars from his gate.*
11. *Poor Lazarus comes a begging at rich Dives' gate, the dogs lick his sores.*
12. *The good angel and death contend for Lazarus' life.*
13. *Rich Dives is taken sick and dieth, he is buried in great solemnity.*
14. *Rich Dives in Hell, and Lazarus in Abraham's bosom*, seen in a most glorious object, all in machines, descending in a throne, guarded with multitudes of angels, with the breaking of the clouds, discovering the palace of the Sun, in double and treble prospects, to the admiration of the spectators.

In the early ages the bishops were accustomed on Christmas Day to sing Carols among the clergy.

Some of the Legendary Carols are very beautiful, and shadow forth the true spirit of our most admired ballad poetry. That entitled the " Holy Well " I would beg to bring forward as a specimen. Although a fragment of an old monkish sermon, or, perhaps, the story of a priest to his simple audience, it is, to my thinking, full of poesy and fine feeling. Jesus, when young, had the ideas and youthful tastes of other children. One day he obtained permission of his mother to play with some little children down by the Holy Well. The juveniles proved to be " lords' and ladies' " sons, and knowing the poverty of Jesus' parents, they objected to his company, and twitted him with the meanness of his birth. Nothing can be more natural than the anger of the indignant mother upon learning the insult. She knows the mighty power of her heavenly boy, but the feelings of a wounded mother's pride are too strong to be suppressed, and she calls upon her son to punish them with his terrible malediction. Jesus' answer is soft and beautiful :—

" Nay, nay," sweet Jesus mildly said,
" Nay, nay, that must not be,
For there are too many sinful souls
Crying out for the help of me."

Books of Carols were cried about the streets of Paris as early as the thirteenth century. In this country we know, from some fragments preserved in the public libraries, that they were published by the first printers.

There also exist numerous old MSS. containing ancient Carols; but these, although they delighted our forefathers when sung by the minstrels, are now almost forgotten. In the time of Henry VIII, and down to the early years of the reign of Charles I, Carols were general at the festive season. When the Puritans came into power, however, an act of parliament was passed, " That no observation shall be had of the 25th day of December, commonly called Christmas Day," and the consequence was that Carols fell into disuse. At the Restoration they once more came into public favour; but, owing to the fondness of Charles for worldly enjoyment, the Carols that were composed and sung at this period are more frequently the subject of noisy mirth and festivity than religion. From this date to the present time the popularity of these joyous songs has been on the wane. Fashions have changed, and tastes have altered; and in this age of giddy excitement people appear to prefer novelty and flippant amusement to the innocent and delightful pastime of their ancient fathers.

Forty years ago an antiquary wrote complainingly:— " Carols begin to be spoken of as not belonging to this century, and yet no one, as I am aware of, has attempted a collection of these fugitives." Several gleaners since then, however, have entered the field. Mr. Davies Gilbert, Mr. Sandys, Dr. Rimbault, and Mr. Thomas Wright have each garnered their gleanings into little volumes. From these I have derived much assistance in the compilation of the present work.

INTRODUCTION.

Much more could have been said in this introduction relative to the history of Carols than has been attempted, but the remarks prefixed to each Carol will be found to contain many particulars concerning our subject. With regard to the date of these pieces most of them may be pronounced ancient,—if not in composition, yet in subject.

The Editor is aware that many of the Carols represent the most indifferent poetry. He was prevailed upon to include them in the collection for various reasons,—their earnest simplicity, the old religious stories they frequently contained, together with a considerable respect for that general favour which for many generations has been accorded to them by all classes.

In collecting materials for the present work it was endeavoured not to include anything contrary to morality or good taste. The Editor has arranged the Carols under the several heads of *Legendary and Narrative; Religious; Numeral; Carols in praise of the Holly and Ivy; Boar's Head Carols;* and a selection of what may be entitled *Festive Carols*—the joyous songs of ancient hospitality and harmless mirth; the blending of festive enjoyment with religion of the heart. In the old days of simple manners it was the custom to hail the season of Christ's birth with a smiling face.

"Man, be merie as bryd on berie, and al thi care let away!"

is the advice prefixed to an ancient Carol in the British Museum.   J. S.

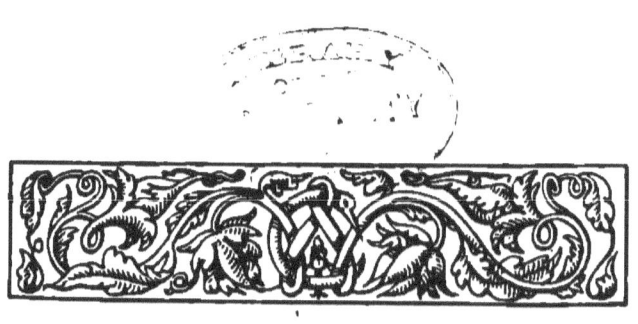

CHRISTMAS CAROLS.

PART I.

LEGENDARY AND NARRATIVE.

CAROL FOR ST. STEPHEN'S DAY.

[THIS Carol is of the beginning of the fifteenth century. The legend itself dates back to a much more remote period. The story of the cock was originally applied to other saints, as St. James, St. Peter, or the Virgin. The oldest account, about 1200, is this:—Two friends sat down to dinner in Bologna, and one bade the other carve the cock, which he did, so that, as he said, not St. Peter or our Lord himself could put it together again. The cock sprang up, clapped his wings and crowed, scattering the sauce over the two friends, and rendering them lepers till the day of their death. The same miracle is related as having occurred to prove the innocence of persons falsely accused, and is found in the legends of Spain, Brittany, Italy, and Sclavonian countries. How it came to be appropriated to St. Stephen does not appear. The boar's head, which he brings in, was the established Yule-tide dish of the North in old heathen times, as well as afterwards.

I am indebted for the above facts to Dr. Prior's delightful volumes of *Danish Ballads*, recently published. That gentleman has given the very curious Danish version of the legend.

In the Carol entitled the *Carnal and the Crane*, further on, this same legend appears in a more modern dress.

Very nearly the original words of this old Carol are given, as a specimen of the language of the period.]

AINT Stephen was a clerk
    In king Herodes hall,
And served him of bread and cloth
    As ever king befalle.[1]

Stephen out of kitchen came
    With boar's head in hande,
He saw a star was fair and bright,
    Over Bethlem stonde.

He cast adown the boar's head,
    And went into the halle;
"I forsake thee, king Herod,
    And thy werkes alle.

"I forsake thee, king Herod,
    And thine werkes alle,
There is a child in Bethlem borne,
    Is better than we alle."

[1] *Befalle*, i. e. happened;—as well as ever happened to a king.

"What aileth thee, Stephen,
   What is thee befalle?
Lacketh thee either meat or drink,
   In king Herod's hall?"

"Lacketh me neither meat nor drink
   In king Herod's hall,
There is a child in Bethlem born,
   Is better than we all."

"What aileth thee, Stephen,
   Art thou wode,[2] or thou ginnest to brede?[3]
Lacketh thee either gold or fee,
   Or any rich weede?"

"Lacketh me neither gold nor fee,
   Nor none rich weede,[4]
There is a child in Bethlem born
   Shall help us at our need."

[2] *Wode*, i. e. mad.
[3] *Brede*, i. e. upbraid. Danish, *bebreide*. In Chaucer the line,—
   "For veray wo out of his wit he braide,"
is explained, "he went or ran out of his wits."
[4] *Weede*, i. e. dress.

"That is all so sooth, Stephen,
  All so sooth, I wiss,
As this capon crow shall,
  That lyeth here in my dish."

That word was not so soon said,
  That word in that hall,
The capon crew, *Christus natus est*,
  Among the lordes all.

Riseth up my tormentors,
  By two, and all by one,
And leadeth Stephen out of town,
  And stoneth him with stone.

Token they Stephen,
  And stoned him in the way,
And therefore is his even,
  On Christes owen day.

THE VIRGIN AND CHILD.

[THE present Carol has been copied from a reprint of the ancient manuscript in the possession of Thomas Wright, Esq. Another version of it will be found in the " Reliquiæ Antiquæ," printed from a MS. in the Advocates' Library, Edinburgh. It may be remarked that there is a gracefulness and tenderness in many of the touches, not often met with in poems of this early date.]

THIS winter's night
   I saw a sight,
      A star as bright as day,
And ever among
A maiden sung,
   Lullay, by by, lullay.

This lovely lady sat and sang, and to her child she said—
" My son, my brother, my father dear, why lyest thou
      thus in hayd—

My sweet bird,
Though it betide
    Thou be not king veray;[1]
But, nevertheless,
I will not cease
    To sing, by by, lullay."

The Child then spake; in his talking, he to his
    mother said—
" It happeneth, mother, I am King, in crib though I
    be laid;
    For angels bright
    Did down alight,
        Thou knowest it is no nay,
    And of that sight
    Thou mayst be light[2]
        To sing, by by, lullay."

" Now, sweet Son, since Thou art King, why art
    Thou laid in stall?
Why not Thou ordain Thy bedding in some great
    King's hall?

[1] In truth.   [2] Quick.

Me thinketh 't is right
That king or knight
    Should be in good array;
And then among
It were no wrong
    To sing, by by, lullay."

"Mary, mother, I am thy child, though I be laid in stall,
Lords and dukes shall worship Me, and so shall kings all;
    Yet shall we see
    That kings three
        Shall come on the twelfth day;
For this behest
Give me thy breast
    And sing, by by, lullay."

"Now tell me, sweet Son, I thee pray, Thou art my love and dear,
How should I keep Thee to Thy pay,[3] and make Thee glad of cheer;
    For all Thy will
    I would fulfill
        Thou knowest full well in fay,[4]

---

[3] Satisfaction.   [4] In truth.

  And for all this
  I will Thee kiss
   And sing, by by, lullay."

" My dear mother, when time it be, take thou Me up aloft,
And set Me upon thy knee, and handle Me full soft;
  And in thy arm
  Thou wilt me warm,
   And keep me night and day;
  If I should weep
  And may not sleep
   Thou sing, by by, lullay."

" Now, sweet Son, since it is so, all things are at Thy will,
I pray thee grant to me a boon, if it be right and skill,[5]
  That child or man,
  That will or can
   Be merry upon my day;
  To bliss them bring,
  And I shall sing
   Lullay, by by, lullay."

[5] Reasonable.

THE THREE KINGS.

[THREE versions of this Carol are known to exist. Two of them have been reprinted by Thomas Wright, Esq. in his collection of Carols, edited for the Percy Society. The following has been perfected from these. The Carol was written in the reign of Henry VII. With regard to the refrain, such choral endings are common in compositions of the period. Several of the Robin Hood ballads exhibit similar peculiarities of rhyming.]

OW is the time of Christmas come,
Together joined are Father and Son,
And with the Holy Ghost are one,
    In fere-a
God send us a new year-a.

  I would now sing, if that I might,
  Of a Child, so fair to sight,
  A maiden bear this winter's night,
      So still-a;
  And as it was his will-a.

There came three kings from Galilee,
To Bethlehem, that fair citie,
To see Him that should ever be
   By right-a;
Lord, and king, and knight-a.

As they went forth with their offering,
They met Herod, that moody king,
He asked them of their coming
   That way-a;
And thus to them 'gan say-a:—

" From whence come ye, you kings three?"
" Out of the East, as you may see,
To seek him that should ever be
   By right-a;
Lord, and king, and knight-a."

" When you to this child have been,
Come you home this way again,
And tell me all that ye have seen,
   I pray-a;
Go not another way-a."

Then of Herod, that moody king,
They took their leave both old and young,
And forth they went with their offering,
   By light-a
Of the star that shone so bright-a.

Till they came to that blissfull place
Where Jesus and his mother was,
There they offered with great solace
   In fere-a ;
Gold, incense and myrrh-a.

When they had their offering made,
As the Holy Ghost them bade,
Then were they both merry and glad
   And light-a ;
It was a good fair sight-a.

Anon, as on their way they went,
The father of heaven an angel sent,
To those three kings that made present,
   That day-a,
Who thus to them did say-a :—

"My Lord doth warn you every one,
By king Herod ye go not home,
For if you do, you will be slain
   Full soon-a;
And woe to you be done-a."

So forth they went another way,
Through the might of God, his lay
As the angel to them did say,
   Full right-a
It was a good fair sight-a.

When they were come to their countree,
Merry and glad they were all three,
Of the sight that they did see
   By night-a;
By the stars shining light-a.

Kneel we now all here adown
To that Lord of great renown,
And pray we in good devotion
   For grace-a,
In Heaven we have a place-a.

THE GOLDEN CAROL OF MELCHIOR, BALTHAZAR, AND GASPAR,

THE THREE KINGS OF COLOGNE.

[LEGENDARY lore has provided for us three notable personages, Gaspar, Melchior, and Balthazar, commonly known as the Magi, who, guided by the star, were present at or shortly after the Nativity; and who survive in history as " The Three Kings of Cologne." These were the wise men who, under the direction of the star, travelled to Bethlehem with their gifts of gold, myrrh, and frankincense—whence the practice of bestowing gifts at the season of the Nativity. Sir Thomas Browne, in his curious work on vulgar errors, was the first amongst us to resolve the mystery of the three Kings of Cologne. " These wise men or kings," says he, " were probably of Arabia, and descended of Abraham by Keturah, who, apprehending the mystery of the star, were by the same conducted into Judea, returned into their own country, and were after baptized by Thomas; thence about three hundred years after, by Helena the Empress, their bodies were translated to Constantinople, thence by Eustatius into Milan, and at last, by Renatus the Bishop, into Cologne (1170), where they are believed at present to remain, their monuments shown unto strangers, and having lost their Arabian titles, are crowned Kings of Cologne." The legend forms the burden of many Carols, but the common English version follows that now given.]

E saw a light shine out afar,
   On Christmas in the morning,
   And straight we knew Christ's Star it was,
   Bright beaming in the morning.
Then did we fall on bended knee,
   On Christmas in the morning,
And prais'd the Lord, who'd let us see
   His glory at its dawning.

Oh! ever thought be of His Name,
   On Christmas in the morning,
Who bore for us both grief and shame,
   Afflictions sharpest scorning.
And may we die, (when death shall come,)
   On Christmas in the morning,
And see in heav'n, our glorious home,
   That Star of Christmas morning.

FOR CHRISTMAS DAY IN THE MORNING.

[THIS is the popular English version of the *Golden Carol*, just given, and details the wanderings of the Magi, or Three Kings. In the original, *Noël*, the French word for Christmas, or Christmas-carol, is corrupted to "Nowell." I have not hesitated to restore the correct rendering. With regard to the three poor Shepherds, alluded to in the second line, Mr. Sandys remarks, that according to some legends the number was four, called Misael, Achael, Cyriacus, and Stephanus, and these, with the names of the Three Kings, were used as a charm to cure the biting of serpents, and other venomous reptiles and beasts. In the seventh of the Chester Mysteries, the Shepherds, who are there but three, have the more homely names of Harvey, Tudd, and Trowle, and are Cheshire or Lancashire boors by birth and habits. Trowle's gift to our Saviour is "a pair of his wife's old hose."]

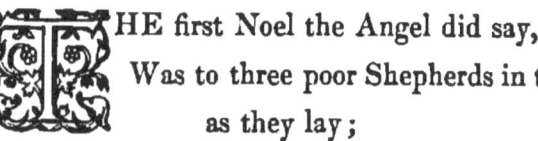HE first Noel the Angel did say,
 Was to three poor Shepherds in the fields
  as they lay;
In the fields where they lay keeping their sheep

In a cold winter's night that was so deep.
    Noel, Noel, Noel, Noel,
    Born is the King of Israel.

They looked up and saw a Star
Shining in the East beyond them far,
And to the earth it gave great light,
And so continued both day and night.
    Noel, &c.

And by the light of that same Star,
Three Wise Men came from land afar;
To seek for a King was their intent,
And to follow the Star wherever it went.
    Noel, &c.

This Star drew nigh to the North West,
O'er Bethlehem it took it's rest,
And there it did both stop and stay
Right over the place where Jesus lay.
    Noel, &c.

Then did they know assuredly
Within that house the King did lie:

One entered in there for to see,
But found the Babe in poverty.
      Noel, &c.

Then enter'd all the Wise Men three
Most reverently upon their knee,
And offer'd there in his prescence,
Both gold, and myrrh, and frankincense.
      Noel, &c.

Now let us all with one accord
Sing praises to our heavenly Lord,
That did make heaven and earth of nought,
But with his blood mankind hath bought.
      Noel, &c.[1]

---

[1] In some old broadside copies two additional, but very foolish verses are occasionally found. They were probably inserted by the local printer when passing his sheet off for "A New Carol."

I SAW THREE SHIPS.

[THIS Carol is sometimes known as *Christmas Day in the Morning*. Hone gives it this title in his list. It has always been a great favourite with the illiterate, and from its quaintness will be found not displeasing to the more refined. Ritson, in his " Introduction to Scotch Songs," vol. 1, gives the following lines as sung during the Christmas holidays about the middle of the sixteenth century, which bear a similarity to this Carol:—

" All sones of Adam, rise up with me,
Go praise the blessed Trinitie, &c.
Then spake the Archangel Gabriel, said, Ave, Mary mild,
The Lord of Lords is with thee, now shall you go with
child.
Ecce ancilla domini.
Then said the Virgin, as thou hast said, so mat it be,
Welcome be heaven's King.
There comes a ship far sailing then,
Saint Michel was the stieres-man;
Saint John sate in the horn:
Our Lord harped, our Lady sang,
And all the bells of heaven they rang,
On Christ's sonday at morn, &c."

There is another version of this Carol common amongst the people which begins—

"As I sat on a sunny bank,
A sunny bank, a sunny bank,
As I sat on a sunny bank,
On Christmas Day in the Morning;"

and finishes with this singular verse—Joseph and his "fair lady" being in the ships—

"O! he did whistle, and she did sing,
And all the bells on earth did ring,
For joy that our Saviour he was born,
On Christmas Day in the Morning."]

I SAW three ships come sailing in,
On Christmas Day, on Christmas Day:
I saw three ships come sailing in
On Christmas Day in the morning.

And who was in those ships all three,
On Christmas Day, on Christmas Day?
And who was in those ships all three,
On Christmas Day in the morning?

Our Saviour Christ and his ladye,
On Christmas Day, on Christmas Day;
Our Saviour Christ and his ladye
On Christmas Day in the morning.

Pray whither sailed those ships all three,
On Christmas Day, on Christmas Day?
Pray whither sailed those ships all three
On Christmas Day in the morning?

O they sailed into Bethlehem,
On Christmas Day, on Christmas Day;
O they sailed into Bethlehem,
On Christmas Day in the morning.

And all the bells on Earth shall ring,
On Christmas Day, on Christmas Day;
And all the bells on Earth shall ring,
On Christmas Day in the morning.

And all the angels in Heaven shall sing,
On Christmas Day, on Christmas Day;
And all the angels in Heaven shall sing,
On Christmas Day in the morning.

And all the souls on Earth shall sing,
On Christmas Day, on Christmas Day;
And all the souls on Earth shall sing,
On Christmas Day in the morning.

Then let us all rejoice amain,
On Christmas Day, on Christmas Day;
Then let us all rejoice amain,
On Christmas Day in the morning.

THE CARNAL AND THE CRANE.

[THE same legend that is given in this Carol is to be observed in the more ancient one to St. Stephen. Ritson has inserted the latter in his *Ancient Ballads*, from an old MS. of the reign of Henry VI.

The *Carnal* is a bird; the word corrupted by the printer into *reign*, is the obsolete word *rein*, formerly used in the sense of *run*. The composition has other marks of age independent of the legend. Hone terms it a Warwickshire Carol.]

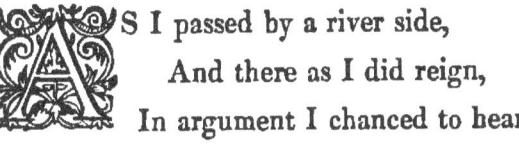S I passed by a river side,
  And there as I did reign,
  In argument I chanced to hear
 A Carnal and a Crane.

 The Carnal said unto the Crane,
  " If all the world should turn,
 Before we had the Father,
  But now we have the Son!

"From whence does the Son come?
    From where and from what place?"
He said, "In a manger,
    Between an ox and an ass!"

"I pray thee," said the Carnal,
    "Tell me before thou go,
Was not the Mother of Jesus
    Conceived by the Holy Ghost?"

"She was a blessed Virgin,
    And pure from all sin;
She was the handmaid of our Lord,
    And Mother of our King."

"Where is the golden cradle
    That Christ was rocked in?
Where are the silken sheets
    That Jesus was wrapt in?"

"A Manger was the cradle
    That Christ was rocked in;
The provender the asses left,
    So sweetly he slept on.

"There was a Star in the West land,
  So bright did it appear
Into King Herod's chamber,
  And where King Herod were.

"The Wise Men soon espied it,
  And told the King on high,
A princely babe was born that night
  No king could e'er destroy.

"'If this be true,' King Herod said,
  'As thou tellest me,
This roasted cock that lies in the dish
  Shall crow full fences[1] three.'

"The cock soon freshly feathered was,
  By the work of God's own hand,
And then three fences crowed he,
  In the dish where he did stand.

"'Rise up, rise up, you merry men all,
  See that you ready be,
All children under two years old
  Now slain they all shall be.'

[1] Shouts?

"Then Jesus, ah! and Joseph,
  And Mary, that was so pure,
They travelled into Egypt,
  As you shall find it sure.

"And when they came to Egypt's Land,
  Among those fierce wild beasts,
Mary, she being weary,
  Must needs sit down to rest.

"'Come sit thee down,' says Jesus,
  'Come sit thee down by me,
And thou shalt see how these wild beasts
  Do come and worship me.'

"First, came the lovely lion,
  Which Jesus's grace did spring,
And of the wild beasts in the field,
  The Lion shall be the king.

"We'll choose our virtuous princes,
  Of birth and high degree,
In every sundry nation,
  Where'er we come and see.

"Then Jesus, ah! and Joseph,
  And Mary, that was unknown,
They travelled by a husbandman,
  Just while his seed was sown.

"'God speed thee, man!' said Jesus,
  'Go fetch thy ox and wain,
And carry home thy corn again,
  Which thou this day hath sown.'

"The husbandman fell on his knees,
  Even before his face;
'Long time hast thou been looked for,
  But now thou art come at last;

"'And I myself do now believe,
  Thy name is Jesus called;
Redeemer of mankind thou art,
  Though undeserving all.'

"'The truth, man, thou hast spoken,
  Of it thou may'st be sure,
For I must lose my precious blood
  For thee and thousands more.

" ' If any one should come this way,
    And enquire for me alone,
Tell them that Jesus passed by,
    When thy seed was sown.'

" After that there came King Herod,
    With his train so furiously,
Enquiring of the husbandman,
    Whether Jesus passed by.

" ' Why the truth it must be spoke,
    And the truth it must be known,
For Jesus passed this way,
    When my seed was sown.

" ' But now I have it reapen,
    And some laid on my wain,
Ready to fetch and carry
    Into my barn again.'

" ' Turn back,' says the Captain,
    ' Your labour and mine's in vain,
It's full three quarters of a year
    Since he his seed has sown.'

"So Herod was deceived
 By the work of God's own hand,
And further he proceeded
 Into the Holy Land.

"There's thousands of children young,
 Which for his sake did die,
Do not forbid these little ones,
 And do not them deny.

"The truth now I have spoken,
 And the truth now I have shown;
How the blessed Virgin,
 She brought us forth a Son."

THE ANGEL GABRIEL FROM GOD.

[THE birth of our Saviour was a mystery upon which the old divines and carolists were ever fond of dwelling. The familiar expressions used towards the Virgin, the angel Gabriel, and the other distinguished personages of the event, served to enlist the sympathies of rustics, and rendered the outlines of the narrative easier to their understanding. In most of the Carols of this kind the plainness of the language employed prevents their being reprinted in any other than in a purely antiquarian work. The following Carol, however, although exhibiting the most indifferent poetry, shadows forth the spirit of its class, and is more free from the objections alluded to than any other I have fallen in with.]

THE Angel Gabriel from God
    Was sent to Galilee,
  Unto a Virgin fair and free,
Whose name was called Mary.
And when the Angel thither came,
  He fell down on his knee,

And looking up in the Virgin's face,
   He said, " All hail, Mary."
      Then, sing we all, both great and small,
         Noel, Noel, Noel;
      We may rejoice to hear the voice
         Of the Angel Gabriel.

Mary anon looked him upon,
   And said, " Sir, what are ye?
I marvel much at these tidings
   Which thou hast brought to me.
Married I am unto an old man,
   As the lot fell unto me;
Therefore I pray depart away,
   For I stand in doubt of thee."
            Then sing, &c.

" Mary," he said, " be not afraid,
   But do believe in me:
The power of the Holy Ghost
   Shall overshadow thee;
Thou shalt conceive without any grief,
   As the Lord told unto me;

God's own dear Son from Heaven shall come,
    And shall be born of thee."
                Then, sing, &c.

This came to pass as God's will was,
    Even as the Angel told.
About midnight an Angel bright
    Came to the Shepherds' fold,
And told them both where and when
    Born was the child, our Lord,
And all along this was their song,
    "All glory be given to God."
                Then, sing, &c.

Good people all, both great and small,
    The which do hear my voice,
With one accord let's praise the Lord,
    And in our hearts rejoice;
Like sister and brother, let's love one another
    Whilst we our lives do spend,
Whilst we have space let's pray for grace,
    And so let my Carol end.
                Then, sing, &c.

THE HOLY WELL.

[THIS popular Carol preserves in quaint and simple verse the outlines of an old legend of the dark ages. The people were anxious to learn more about the first years of the life of Jesus than the Scriptures supplied, and the priests and monks invented various pleasing stories to amuse and instruct them. The Apocryphal Books of the New Testament, also, afforded a great many religious tales. Some of these were put into verse. A specimen may be seen in the following. On the broad-sheet (printed at Gravesend in the last century), it is stated to be " A very Ancient Carol."]

S it fell out one May morning,[1]
And on a bright holiday,
Sweet Jesus asked of his dear mother,
If he might go to play.

[1] I might mention, as an indication of the probable date of this simple composition, that several ballads of the reigns of Henry VIII. and Elizabeth began in this style—

" As it fell out on a holiday,
As it fell out on a Whitsunday," &c.

The whole piece has a strong ballad flavour.

"To play, to play, sweet Jesus shall go,
And to play now get you gone,
And let me hear of no complaint,
At night when you come home."

Sweet Jesus went down to yonder town,
As far as the Holy Well,
And there did see as fine children
As any tongue can tell.

He said, " God bless you every one,
May Christ your portion be;
Little children, shall I play with you?
And you shall play with me."

But they made answer to him, " No,"
They were lords' and ladies' sons;
And he, the meanest of them all,
Was born in an ox's stall.

Sweet Jesus turned him around,
And he neither laugh'd nor smil'd,
But the tears came trickling from his eyes
Like water from the skies.

Sweet Jesus turned him about,
To his mother's dear home went he,
And said, " I have been in yonder town,
As after you may see.

" I have been in yonder town,
As far as the Holy Well;
There did I meet as fine children
As any tongue can tell.

" I bid God bless them every one,
And Christ their bodies see;
Little children, shall I play with you?
And you shall play with me.

" But then they answered me, ' No,'
They were lords' and ladies' sons;
And I, the meanest of them all,
Was born in an ox's stall."

" Though you are but a maiden's child,
Born in an ox's stall,
Thou art the Christ, the King of heaven,
And the Saviour of them all.

"Sweet Jesus, go down to yonder town,
As far as the Holy Well,
And take away those sinful souls,
And dip them deep in hell."

"Nay, nay," sweet Jesus mildly said,
"Nay, nay, that must not be,
For there are too many sinful souls
Crying out for the help of me."

ALL YOU THAT ARE TO MIRTH INCLINED.

[THIS rude old Carol is still an especial favourite with the peasantry. Hone mentions it in his list, and I find that nearly all the broadside printers include it in their yearly sheets. The word "mirth" was certainly not used by the author in that irreverent sense which it now usually conveys. Religious joy was intended, not boisterous merriment. In an old edition of Deloney's Garland of Good-will, this Carol is given under the title of "The Sinner's Redemption."]

ALL you that are to mirth inclined,
Consider well and bear in mind
What our good God for us hath done
In sending his beloved son.

  And to redeem our souls from thrall,
  He is the Saviour of us all.

Let all your songs and praises be
Unto his Heavenly Majesty,

And evermore among your mirth
Remember Christ our Saviour's birth.
     And to redeem, &c.

The five-and-twentieth of December,
Good cause have you for to remember,
In Bethlehem upon this morn
There was our blessed Saviour born.
     And to redeem, &c.

The night before that happy tide
The spotless Virgin, and her guide,
Went long time seeking up and down,
To find them lodging in the town.
     And to redeem, &c.

And mark how all things came to pass,
The inns and lodgings so filled was,
That they could have no room at all,
But in a silly[1] ox's stall.
     And to redeem, &c.

---

[1] Old word for *simple* or *inoffensive*.

That night the Virgin Mary mild
Was safe delivered of a Child,
According unto Heaven's decree
Man's sweet salvation for to be.
     And to redeem, &c.

Near Bethlehem did Shepherds keep
Their herds and flocks, and feeding sheep,
To whom God's Angels did appear,
Which put the Shepherds in great fear.
     And to redeem, &c.

" Prepare and go," the Angel said,
" To Bethlehem, be not afraid;
There shall you see this blessed morn,
The princely babe, sweet Jesus, born."
     And to redeem, &c.

With thankful hearts and joyful mind,
The Shepherds went this Babe to find,
And as the heavenly Angel told,
They did our Saviour Christ behold.
     And to redeem, &c.

Within a manger was he laid,
The Virgin Mary by him stayed,
Attending on the Lord of life,
Being both mother, maid, and wife.
     And to redeem, &c.

Three Eastern Wise Men from afar,
Directed by a glorious Star,
Came boldly on, and made no stay
Until they came where Jesus lay.
     And to redeem, &c.

And being come unto the place
Wherein the blest Messias was,
They humbly laid before his feet
Their gifts of gold and odours sweet.
     And to redeem, &c.

See how the Lord of Heaven and Earth
Shew'd himself lowly in his birth,
A sweet example for mankind,
To learn to bear an humble mind.
     And to redeem, &c.

No costly robes or rich attire
Did Jesus Christ our Lord desire.
No musick nor sweet harmony,
Till glorious Angels came from high.
    And to redeem, &c.

If choirs of Angels did rejoice,
Well may mankind with heart and voice
Sing praises to the God of Heaven,
That unto us his Son is given.
    And to redeem, &c.

GLORIA TIBI, DOMINE.

[SINGING short stories of the birth of our Saviour as Carol-lullabys to infants appears to have been common in early times. In those ages no occasion seems to have been lost sight of for narrating impressive portions of the story of Christ. Rhyming narratives of the wicked Herod, and the poor little infants, were also general in the nurseries. Portions of these lullabys tacked to hymns, or carols altered to suit the infant comprehension, are now occasionally met with.

Latin choruses to Godly Songs or Carols in the vernacular arose from the use of Latin prayers and chants in the churches in those days. Education, prior to the Reformation, being for the most part conducted at or under supervision of the monasteries, Monkish Latin was tolerably familiar to the people.]

HERE is a Child born of our blessed
Virgin;
I heard a Maid lullaby to sing:
" Peace, my dear Child, of thy weeping,
For thou shalt be our Heavenly King."
Now sing we, and now sing we,
To the Gloria tibi, Domine.

"O Mother! O Mother! your wishes are nought;
　It is not for me such carols are wrought;
Such carols were never by woman thought
　　To the Gloria tibi, Domine."
　　　　　　　　　Now sing we, &c.

"O my dear Son, why sayest thou so?
Thou art my Son, I have no moe;
When Gabriel bespoke thee full of grace,
Thou needest not to tell me of this case."
　　　　　　　　　Now sing we, &c.

"O, they will thrust, Mother, my head from my hair,
With a crown of sharp thorns they me will not
　　　spare,
And with sharp spears my heart will tear,
　　To the Gloria tibi, Domine.
　　　　　　　　　Now sing we, &c.

"O come you here, Mother, and you shall see
My hands and feet nailed to the rood tree,
And my feet, Mother, are fastened thereby,
A vile sight, Mother, for you to see."

Now sing we, and now sing we,
To the Gloria tibi, Domine,
And now sing we more or less,
And welcome be this merry Christmas.

THE CHERRY-TREE CAROL.

[MARY's desire for the fruit on the cherry-tree, and Joseph's refusal to gather it for her on the return of his jealousy, a singular legend of the dark ages, forms the subject of a Christmas Carol still sung in many parts of the country. The remarkable scene occurs in the fifteenth pageant of the "Coventry Mysteries." *Mary* says (I give the original phraseology):—

    Amy swete husbond, wolde ye telle to me
    What tre is yon standynge upon yon hylle?
Joseph. Forsothe, Mary, it is clepyd a chery tre,
    In time of yer ye myght fede you ỹ on yõ fylle.

Maria. Turne ageyn husbond and beholde yon tre,
    How y^t blomyght now so swetely.
Joseph. Cum on, Mary y^t we worn at yon cyte,
    Or ellys we may be blamyd I telle yow lythly.

Maria. Now my spouse, I pray you to be hold
    How ye cheryes growyn upon yon tre,
    For to have ỹ of ryght fayn I wold,
    & it plesyd yow to labor so mech for me.

Joseph. Yo^r desyr to fulfylle I shal assay sekyrly,
    Ow to plucke you of these cheries it is a werk wylde,

>   For ye tre is so hyg it wold not be lyghtly,
>   Ȳ for lete hȳ pluk yon cheryes be gatt you wᵗ childe.
>
> *Maria.* Now good Lord I pray the, graunt me yis boun,
>   To have of yese cheries, and it be yoʳ wylle,
>   Now I thank it God, yis tre bowyth to me down.
>   I may now gaderȳ anowe & eten my fylle.
>
> *Joseph.* Ow, I know weyl I have offended my God ī trinyte,
>   Spekeyng to my spowse these unkynde wurdys,
>   For now I believe wel it may now other be
>   But yᵗ my spowse beryght yᵉ kyngs son of blys, &c.

A writer on Carols has remarked, " the admiration of my earliest days, for some lines in the 'Cherry Carol' still remains, nor can I help thinking that the reader will see somewhat of cause for it." Different versions, with additions and omissions, are given in the modern broadsides. The version here printed has been made after a careful examination of several copies printed in various parts of England. A few verses it was thought advisable to omit, but the sequence of the narrative is supplied by prose explanations.]

JOSEPH was an old man,
  And an old man was he,
  When he married Mary
The Queen of Galilee.

Joseph and Mary walked
 Through a garden gay,
Where the cherries they grew
 Upon every tree.

> Joseph and Mary walked
> Through an orchard good,
> Where were cherries and berries
> As red as any blood.[1]

Joseph, upon learning that the union with his " cousin Mary" is about to be blessed by a babe, suddenly becomes jealous and unkind. The Carol continues:—

> O then bespoke Mary,
> With words both meek and mild,
> " Gather me some cherries, Joseph,
> They run so in my mind."

The next verse gives Joseph's uncouth answer, that if she wants cherries she must ask somebody else to gather them for her, as he is not inclined to do so. The spirit of the unborn Jesus, however, hears the rebuke, and he commands his mother:—

> " Go to the tree, Mary,
> And it shall bow to thee,
> And the highest branch of all
> Shall bow down to Mary's knee.

[1] Other copies of this Carol supply different versions of these verses. One printed at Birmingham reads:—

> " Joseph and Mary walked
> In the garden gay,
> Where exercises grew
> Upon every spray," &c.

"Go to the tree, Mary,
    And it shall bow to thee,
And you shall gather cherries,
    By one, by two, and three."

Then bowed down the highest tree
    Unto his Mother's hand:
"See," Mary cried, "see, Joseph,
    I have cherries at command!"[2]

Joseph relents at the harsh words he has spoken, and replies:—

"O eat your cherries, Mary,
    O eat your cherries now,
O eat your cherries, Mary,
    That grow upon the bough."[3]

---

[2] Another version represents the fruit as previously ordained for Mary:—
"'Now you may see, Joseph,
Those cherries were for me.'"

[3] The version given by Mr. Sandys reads:—
"O then bespake Joseph,
'I have done Mary wrong,
But cheer up, my dearest,
And be not cast down.'"

Mr. Sandys obtained the Carol from the West country, where everybody, even strangers, are addressed as "my dear."

Time is supposed to have elapsed, and the scene has changed.

> As Joseph was a walking
>   He heard an angel sing :—
> " This night shall be born
>   Our Heavenly King ;
>
> " He neither shall be born
>   In housen, nor in hall,
> Nor in the place of Paradise,
>   But in an ox's stall ;
>
> " He neither shall be clothed,
>   In purple nor in pall
> But all in fair linen,
>   As were babies all ;
>
> " He neither shall be rocked
>   In silver nor in gold,
> But in a wooden cradle,
>   That rocks on the mould ;
>
> " He neither shall be christened
>   In white wine nor red,
> But with fair spring water
>   With which we were christened."

More time has elapsed, and the scene again changes.

> Then Mary took her young Son,
>   And set him on her knee :—
> "I pray thee now, dear child,
>   Tell how this world shall be?"

> "O, I shall be as dead, Mother,
>   As the stones in the wall;
> O, the stones in the street, Mother,
>   Shall mourn for me all.[4]

> "And upon a Wednesday
>   My vow I will make,
> And upon Good Friday
>   My death I will take;

> "Upon Easter-day, Mother,
>   My uprising shall be;
> O, the sun and the moon, Mother,
>   Shall both rise with me."

[4] The Warwickshire broadside copy in my possession gives this stanza :—

> "This world shall be like
>   The stones in the street,
> For the sun and the moon
>   Shall bow down at my feet."

DIVES AND LAZARUS.

[This Carol, I believe, has not been given in any previous collection. It is reprinted here from an old Birmingham broadside. Hone appears to have met with it, and alludes to a quaint rendering of the thirteenth verse which occurred in his copy. The lines are—

> " Rise up, rise up, brother Dives,
> And come along with me,
> For you've a place provided in hell
> To sit upon a serpent's knee."

The idea of sitting on the serpent's knee was, perhaps, conveyed to the poet's mind by old woodcut representations of Lazarus seated in Abraham's lap. More anciently, Abraham was frequently drawn holding him up by the sides that he might be the better seen by Dives in the fiery pit.]

AS it fell out upon a day,
    Rich Dives he made a feast,
    And he invited all his friends,
And gentry of the best.

Then Lazarus laid him down and down,
    And down at Dives' door,
" Some meat, some drink, brother Dives,
    Bestow upon the poor."

" Thou art none of my brother, Lazarus,
    That lies begging at my door,
No meat nor drink will I give thee,
    Nor bestow upon the poor."

Then Lazarus laid him down and down,
    And down at Dives's wall,
" Some meat, some drink, brother Dives,
    Or with hunger starve I shall."

" Thou art none of my brother, Lazarus,
    That lies begging at my wall,
No meat nor drink will I give thee,
    But with hunger starve you shall."

Then Lazarus laid him down and down,
    And down at Dives's gate,
" Some meat, some drink, brother Dives,
    For Jesus Christ his sake."

"Thou art none of my brother, Lazarus,
　That lies begging at my gate,
No meat nor drink will I give thee,
　For Jesus Christ his sake."

Then Dives sent out his merry men,
　To whip poor Lazarus away,
They had no power to strike a stroke,
　But flung their whips away.

Then Dives sent out his hungry dogs,
　To bite him as he lay,
They had no power to bite at all,
　But licked his sores away.

As it fell out upon a day,
　Poor Lazarus sickened and died,
There came two angels out of heaven,
　His soul therein to guide.

"Rise up, rise up, brother Lazarus,
　And go along with me,
For you've a place prepared in heaven,
　To sit on an angel's knee."

As it fell out upon a day,
   Rich Dives sickened and died,
There came two serpents out of hell,
   His soul therein to guide.

" Rise up, rise up, brother Dives,
   And go with us to see,
A dismal place prepared in hell,
   From which thou canst not flee."

Then Dives looked up with his eyes,
   And saw poor Lazarus blest,
" Give me one drop of water, brother Lazarus,
   To quench my flaming thirst.

" Oh! had I as many years to abide,
   As there are blades of grass,
Then there would be an end, but now
   Hell's pains will ne'er be past.

" Oh! was I now but alive again,
   The space of one half hour,
Oh! that I had my peace secure,
   Then the devil should have no power."

THE MOON SHINES BRIGHT.

[As in the case of some of the preceding, there are, doubtless, expressions in this simple effusion at which it is difficult to abstain from smiling. The perfect earnestness of these Carols, however, and the charm they have long held over the people, are sufficient apologies for inserting them here. Often they are the sole vehicles of ancient religious stories that have come down to us in this form when they have perished in the more dignified chronicles. On a broadside copy printed about 1750, I observe that it is entitled " A New Christmas Carol;" but I scarcely think it was composed later than the early part of the preceding century.]

THE moon shines bright, and the stars give
    a light,
  A little before it was day,
Our Lord, our God, he called on us,
  And bid us awake and pray.

  Awake, awake, good people all,
    Awake and you shall hear,

Our Lord, our God, he died on the cross,
    For us whom he loved so dear.

O fair, O fair Jerusalem,
    When shall I come to thee?
When shall my sorrows have an end,
    Thy joy that I may see?

The fields were green as green could be,
    When from his glorious seat
Our Lord, our God, he watered us,
    With his heavenly dew so sweet.

And for the saving of our souls
    Christ died upon the cross;
We ne'er shall do for Jesus Christ
    As he has done for us.

The life of man is but a span,
    And cut down in its flower,
We are here to-day and to-morrow are gone,
    We are all dead in an hour.

O pray teach your children, man,
 The while that you are here;
It will be better for your souls
 When your corpse lies on the bier.

With one turf at your head, O man,
 And another at your feet,
Thy good deeds and thy bad, O man,
 Will altogether meet.

My song is done, I must begone,
 I can stay no longer here,
God bless you all both great and small,
 And send you a joyful new year!

GOD REST YOU MERRY GENTLEMEN.

[THIS is perhaps the greatest favourite of all the Carols now sung at Christmas. The melody is homely and plaintive, and appears to touch that chord in the popular mind which more elaborate compositions appeal to in vain. An antiquary many years ago thus spoke of it :—" The melody of ' *God rest you Merry Gentlemen*' delighted my childhood, and I still listen with pleasure (as who does not) to the shivering carolist's evening chant towards the clear kitchen window deck'd with holly, the flaring fire showing the whitened hearth and reflecting gleams of light from the surfaces of the dresser utensils."

An old broadside copy of this, with three other " choice Carols for Christmas Holidays," occurs in the Roxburge Collection in the British Museum. Mr. Chappell, in his valuable work on " *Popular Music*," presents us with two versions of the tune, and adds, " I have received many others from different sources, for no carol seems to be more generally known."]

GOD rest you merry gentlemen,
    Let nothing you dismay,
    For Jesus Christ, our Saviour,
Was born upon this day ;

To save us all from Satan's power,
   When we were gone astray.
      O tidings of comfort and joy,
         For Jesus Christ, our Saviour, was born on
            Christmas Day.

In Bethlehem, in Jewry
   This blessed babe was born,
And laid within a manger
   Upon this blessed morn;
The which His mother Mary
   Nothing did take in scorn.
               O tidings, &c.

From God, our Heavenly Father,
   A blessed Angel came,
And unto certain shepherds,
   Brought tidings of the same;
How that in Bethlehem was born
   The Son of God by name.
               O tidings, &c.

" Fear not," then said the Angel,
   " Let nothing you affright,

This day is born a Saviour,
   Of virtue, power, and might.
So frequently to vanish all
   The friends of Satan quite."
                    O tidings, &c.

The shepherds, at those tidings,
   Rejoiced much in mind,
And left their flocks a-feeding
   In tempest, storm, and wind,
And went to Bethlehem straightway
   The Son of God to find.
                    O tidings, &c.

But when to Bethlehem they came,
   Where as this Infant lay,
They found Him in a manger,
   Where oxen feed on hay,
His mother Mary kneeling
   Unto the Lord did pray.
                    O tidings, &c.

Now to the Lord sing praises,
   All you within this place,

And with true love and brotherhood
Each other now embrace,
This holy tide of Christmas
All others doth deface.

O tidings, &c.[1]

[1] With regard to the text of this Carol I may remark that nearly every town in England, at each succeeding Christmas, supplies us with variations. The above appeared the most genuine.

A VIRGIN MOST PURE.

[This Carol exhibits traces of antiquity, but nothing certain regarding its history can be learnt. It has enjoyed great popularity for many years, being found on nearly all single collections of Carols. Throughout the West it is a great favourite. A different version from that given below occurs on an old broadside printed at Birmingham in my possession. The first verse begins :—

"A virgin unspotted the prophets foretold,
Should bring forth a Saviour which now we behold,
To be our Redeemer from death, hell, and sin,
Which Adam's transgression involved us in."]

A VIRGIN most pure, as the Prophets do tell,
Hath brought forth a Babe, as it hath befell,
To be our Redeemer from death, hell, and sin,
Which by Adam's transgression hath wrapt us all in.
    Rejoice and be you merry, set sorrow aside,
    Christ Jesus our Saviour was born on this tide.

In Bethlehem city, in Jury it was,—
Where Joseph and Mary together did pass,
And there to be taxed, with many one more,
For Cæsar commanded the same should be so.
        Rejoice, &c.

But when they had entered the city so fair,
The number of people so mighty was there,
That Joseph and Mary, whose substance was small,
Could get in the city no lodging at all.
        Rejoice, &c.

Then they were constrained in a stable to lie,
Where oxen and asses they used to tie;
Their lodging so simple, they held it no scorn,
But against the next morning our Saviour was born.
        Rejoice, &c.

The King of all Glory to the world being brought,
Small store of fine linen to wrap him was brought;
When Mary had swaddled her young Son so sweet,
Within an ox manger she laid him to sleep.
        Rejoice, &c.

Then God sent an Angel from heaven so high,
To certain poor shepherds in fields where they lie,
And bid them no longer in sorrow to stay,
Because that our Saviour was born on this day.
Rejoice, &c.

Then presently after, the shepherds did spy
A number of Angels appear in the sky,
Who joyfully talked, and sweetly did sing,
" To God be all Glory, our Heavenly King."
Rejoice, &c.

· Three certain Wise Princes, they thought it most
    meet,
To lay their rich offerings at our Saviour's feet ;
Then the shepherds consented, and to Bethlehem
    did go,
And when they came thither, they found it was so.
Rejoice, &c.

THE WORCESTERSHIRE CAROL.

[I CANNOT find this Carol in any printed collection that I have examined. Hone does not mention it in his extensive list. It occurs on an old broadsheet printed at Birmingham in my collection. Apart from its exceeding grandiloquence it will be found to contain many quaint touches, and pleasing lines. The date is apparently sometime during the last century.]

HOW grand and how bright,
    That wonderful night,
      When angels to Bethlehem came,
  They burst forth like fires,
  They struck their gold lyres,
And mingled their sound with the flame.

    The shepherds were amazed,
    The pretty lambs gazed,
At darkness thus turned into light,
    No voice was there heard,

From man, beast, or bird,
So sudden and solemn the sight.

And then when the sound
Re-echoed around,
The hills and the dales all awoke,
The moon and the stars
Stopt their fiery ears,
And listened while Gabriel spoke :—

" I bring you," said he,
" From the glorious tree,
A message both gladsome and good,
The Saviour is come
To the world as his home,
But he lies in a manger of wood."

At mention of this,
The source of all bliss,
The angels sang loudly and long,
They soared to the sky,
Beyond mortal eye,
But left us the words of their song :—

"All glory to God,
Who laid by his rod,
To smile on the world through his Son,
And peace be on earth,
For this wonderful birth
Most wonderful conquests has won.

"And good will to man,
Though his life's but a span,
And his soul all sinful and vile."
Then pray, Christians, pray,
And let Christmas Day
Have a tear as well as a smile.

COME REJOICE, ALL GOOD CHRISTIANS.

[APART from their antiquity, the quaint simplicity of these lines is again the only recommendation that can be urged for giving them a place in this collection. This Carol, which has long been a favourite, may be met with in most popular or street collections at the festive season.]

COME rejoice, all good Christians,
 And rejoice now, I pray,
For joy our Redeemer
Was born on this day,
In the city of David,
 At a cottage so poor :
Then rejoice and be you merry,
 We have blessings in store.
   And therefore be you merry,
   Rejoice and be you merry,

Set sorrows away,
Christ Jesus, our Saviour,
Was born on this day.

Our Lord he was born
  Of a Virgin most pure,
Within a poor stable
  Both safe and secure.
He was guarded most safely
  With Angels so bright,
Who told three poor Shepherds
  Those things in the night.
        And therefore, &c.

They said, " Be not fearful,
  But to Bethlehem go ;
Then rejoice and be cheerful
  For 'tis certainly so.
For a young son to Joseph
  Is in Bethlehem born,
Then rejoice, all good Christians,
  And cease for to mourn."
        And therefore, &c.

And when those three Shepherds
　　Did to Bethlehem come,
And arrived at the Stable,
　　Then in they did run.
Where they found blessed Mary
　　With Jesus her Son :
There they found our Lord sleeping,
　　And thus they begun.
　　　　　　　And therefore, &c.

With the sweetest Hallelujah
　　The Heavens did rejoice,
With the Saints and the Angels,
　　And all with sweet voice,
Crying, " Glory and honour
　　To our Heavenly King !"
In the clouds of the air
　　Then this Host they did sing.
　　　　　　　And therefore, &c.

　　Then well may we Christians,
　　　　That dwell on the earth,
　　Rejoice and be glad
　　　　For sweet Jesus his birth,

Who brought us salvation,
    If we mind but the same:
Then let all in the nation
    Sing praise to his name.
        And therefore, &c.

With true zeal and honour
    Let us joyfully sing,
In praise of our salvation,
    To our Heavenly King:
To our Heavenly Father,
    That remaineth above,
And to our dear Saviour,
    That redeem'd us with love.
        And therefore, &c.

THE SEVEN VIRGINS.

[THIS is another Carol which has hitherto eluded the search of all collectors of such religious antiquities. The legend is extremely ancient. The line towards the end which alludes to " our king and queen" is evidently a modern interpolation. The metre, occasionally faulty, is here given just as it occurs on the original old Birmingham broadside.]

ALL under the leaves, and the leaves of life,
 I met with virgins seven,
And one of them was Mary mild,
 Our Lord's mother of heaven.

" O what are you seeking, you seven fair maids,
 All under the leaves of life,
Come tell, come tell, what seek you,
 All under the leaves of life?"

"We're seeking for no leaves, Thomas,
  But for a friend of thine,
We're seeking for sweet Jesus Christ,
  To be our guide and thine."

"Go down, go down to yonder town,
  And sit in the gallery,
And there you'll see sweet Jesus Christ,
  Nailed to a big yew tree."

So down they went to yonder town,
  As fast as foot could fall,
And many a grievous bitter tear,
  From the virgins' eyes did fall.

"O peace, mother, O peace, mother,
  Your weeping doth me grieve,
I must suffer this," he said,
  "For Adam and for Eve."

"O mother, take you John Evangelist,
  All for to be your son,
And he will comfort you sometimes,
  Mother, as I have done."

"O come, thou John Evangelist,
   Thou'rt welcome unto me,
But more welcome my own dear Son,
   Whom I nursed on my knee."

Then he laid his head on his right shoulder,
   Seeing death it struck him nigh,—
"The Holy Ghost be with your soul,
   I die, mother dear, I die."

O the rose, the gentle rose,
   And the fennel that grows so green,
God give us grace, in every place,
   To pray for our king and queen.

Furthermore for our enemies all
   Our prayers they should be strong,
Amen, good Lord; your Charity
   Is the ending of my song.

LAST NIGHT AS I LAY SLEEPING.

[THE old religious belief that a guardian angel was appointed to watch over each bed, and that he occasionally held intercourse with the occupant, here forms the machinery of a Carol. The composition probably dates back several generations. It is now immediately taken from an old Carol-sheet, never before having been included in a collection.]

LAST night as I lay sleeping,
    When all my prayers were said,
With my guardian angel keeping
    His watch above my head;
I heard his sweet voice caroling,
    Full softly on my ear,
A song for Christian boys to sing,
    For Christian men to hear.

"Thy body be at rest, dear boy,
    Thy soul be free from sin;

I'll shield thee from the world's annoy,
   And breathe pure words within.
The holy Christmas tide is nigh,
   The season of Christ's birth:
Glory be to God on high,
   And peace to men on earth.

" Myself and all the heavenly host
   Were keeping watch of old,
And saw the shepherds at their posts,
   And all the sheep in fold.
Then told we with a joyful cry,
   The tidings of Christ's birth;
Glory be to God on high,
   And peace to men on earth.

" He bowed to all his Father's will,
   And meek he was and lowly;
And year by year his thoughts were still
   Most innocent and holy.
He did not come to strive or cry,
   But ever from his birth,
Gave glory unto God on high,
   And peace to men on earth.

"Like him be true, like him be pure,
  Like him be full of love;
Seek not thine own, and so secure
  Thine own that is above.
And still when Christmas tide draws nigh,
  Sing thou of Jesus' birth:
Glory be to God on high,
  And peace to men on earth."

Part II.

RELIGIOUS CAROLS.

"IN EXCELSIS GLORIA."

[Bishop Taylor was of the opinion that the "Gloria in Excelsis," the hymn sung by the angels to the Shepherds at our Lord's Nativity, was the earliest Christmas Carol. It is preserved in an old MS. among the Harleian collection in the British Museum, supposed to have been written about the year 1500. In English Carols of this antiquity Latin words and even whole lines are freely interlarded. They are composite or macaronic in their language; and the refrain of this curious piece, "*In Excelsis Gloria*"—Glory in the highest—is retained in its original form, doubtless, from its analogy to the "gloria" which the priests were accustomed to intone at the altar.

The "Gloria in Excelsis" is sung in Roman Catholic chapels on the Holy Thursday, Holy Saturday, and at midnight on Christmas Even, and then again at eleven o'clock on Christmas Morning.]

WHEN Christ was born of Mary free,
In Bethlehem in that fair citie,
Angels sang there with mirth and glee,
In Excelsis Gloria !

Herdsmen beheld these angels bright,
To them appearing with great light,
Who said, " God's Son is born this night,"
In Excelsis Gloria !

This King is come to save mankind,
As in Scripture truths we find,
Therefore this song have we in mind,
In Excelsis Gloria !

Then, dear Lord, for Thy great Grace,
Grant us the bliss to see Thy face,
That we may sing to Thy solace,
In Excelsis Gloria !

WELCOME YULE.

[THIS early Carol (temp. Henry VI.) given by Ritson in his *Ancient Songs and Ballads*, with its mixture of Scriptural allusions and invitations to worldly enjoyment, was, doubtless, one of those sung by the tribe of professional minstrels during the several periods of feasting into which the day of Yule was divided. It was thought at first that it could scarcely be classed as religious, yet was that element found so predominant that it has been included in this part.]

ELCOME be thou heavenly King;
Welcome, born on this morning,
Welcome, for whom we shall sing
  Welcome Yule.[1]

Welcome be ye Stephen and John,
Welcome Innocents every one,
Welcome Thomas Martyr one,
  Welcome Yule.

[1] *Yule* is the Anglo-Saxon for Christmas.

Welcome be ye good New Year,
Welcome Twelfth day both in fere,[2]
Welcome Saints loved and dear,
        Welcome Yule.

Welcome be ye Candlemass,
Welcome be ye Queen of Bliss,
Welcome both to more and less,[3]
        Welcome Yule.

Welcome be ye that are here,
Welcome all, and make good cheer,
Welcome all, another year,
        Welcome Yule.

[2] In company.   [3] Great and small.

A CAROL ON THE BIRTH OF CHRIST.

[This Carol was written by Thomas Tusser, the author of the well-known work on Husbandry. Hs was chorister and agriculturist by turns. The poems that he has left us are noted for their morality, piety, and benevolent simplicity. Tusser died in 1580.]

WAS not Christ our Saviour
    Sent unto us from God above,
    Not for our good behaviour,
But only of his mercy and love?
If this be true, as true it is,
    Truly indeed ;
Great thanks to God to yield for this
    Then had we need.

This did our God for very troth,
    To train to Him the soul of man,

And justly to perform his oath
    To Sarah, and to Abraham, than
That through his seed, all nations should
      Most blessed be,
As in due time performed, He would
      All flesh should see.

Which wondrously is brought to pass,
    And in our sight already done,
By sending as his promise was
    (To comfort us) His only Son,
Even Christ, I mean, that virgin's child
      In Bethlehem born :
That Lamb of God, that Prophet mild,
      With crowned thorn.

Such was His love, to save us all,
    From dangers of the curse of God,
That we stood in by Adam's fall,
    And by our own deserved rod.
That through His blood and holy name,
      All that believe,
And fly from sin, and abhor the same,
      Shall grace receive.

For this glad news, this feast doth bring,
  To God the Son and Holy Ghost,
Let man give thanks, rejoice and sing,
  From world to world, from coast to coast,
For other gifts in many ways,
    That God doth send:
Let us in Christ give God the praise,
    Till life shall end.

CAROL, WITH LULLABY.

[This Carol is taken from "Tenor Psalmes, Sonets, and Songs of Sadnes and Pietie, made into Musicke of Five Parts, &c. by William Byrd, one of the Gent. of the Queenes Maiestie's Royall Chappell, &c. London, 1587," and printed therefrom in " Cens. Liter." vol. x. pp. 187-8. Herod's cruel massacre is a common subject in children's Carols.]

LULLA, la lulla, lulla lullaby,
    My sweet little babe, what meanest thou
        to cry?
Be still, my blessed babe, though cause thou hast to
    mourn,
Whose blood, most innocent, the cruel king hath
    sworn:
And lo, alas, behold what slaughter he doth make,
Shedding the blood of infants all, sweet Saviour, for
    Thy sake,

A King is born, they say, which King this king
    would kill;
Oh wo, and woful heavy day, when wretches have
    their will.

Lulla, la lulla, lulla lullaby,
My sweet little babe, what meanest thou to cry?
Three kings this King of kings to see, are come from
    far,
To each unknown, with offerings great, by guiding
    of a star!
And Shepherds heard the song, which angels bright
    did sing,
Giving all glory unto God, for coming of this King.
Which must be made away, King Herod would
    Him kill;
Oh wo, and woful heavy day, when wretches have
    their will.

Lulla, la lulla, lulla lullaby,
My sweet little babe, what meanest thou to cry?
Lo, my little babe, be still, lament no more,
From fury shall thou step aside, help have we still in
    store;

We heavenly warning have, some other soil to seek,
From death must fly the Lord of Life, as lamb both
    mild and meek :
Thus must my babe obey the king that would him
    kill,
Oh wo, and woful heavy day, when wretches have
    their will.

    Lulla, la lulla, lulla lullaby,
My sweet little babe, what meanest thou to cry?
But thou shalt live and reign, as sybils have foresaid,
As all the prophets prophesy, whose mother, yet a maid,
And perfect virgin pure, with her breasts shall up-breed
Both God and man, that all have made the Son of
    heavenly seed;
Whom caitiffs none can 'tray, whom tyrants none
    can kill,
Oh joy, and joyful happy day, when wretches want
    their will.

NEW PRINCE, NEW POMP.

[ROBERT SOUTHWELL, the writer of the following poem, is chiefly remembered on account of his unfortunate fate. He was educated for the Catholic priesthood, and when young became a member of the Society of Jesus at Rome. After a time he returned to his own country in the character of a missionary. But he found the government adverse to his Order. For eight years he managed to escape the particular notice of the authorities, but at length he was arrested, and thrown into prison, where he endured the torture of the rack ten times. Eventually he was executed at Tyburn, February 21, 1595.]

BEHOLD a silly[1] tender Babe,
   In freezing winter night,
   In homely manger trembling lies;
Alas! a piteous sight.
The inns are full, no man will yield
   This little Pilgrim bed;

[1] This expression frequently occurs in ancient Carols. It meant in those days *artless, simple*.

But forced He is with silly beasts,
In crib to shroud His head.
Despise Him not for lying here,
First what He is inquire:
An orient pearl is often found
In depth of dirty mire.
Weigh not His crib, His wooden dish,
  Nor beasts that by Him feed:
Weigh not His mother's poor attire,
Nor Joseph's simple weed.
This stable is a Prince's court,
  The crib His chair of state;
The beasts are parcel of His pomp,
  The wooden dish His plate;
The persons in that poor attire,
  His royal liveries wear;
The Prince himself is come from Heaven,
  This pomp is prizèd there.
With joy approach, O Christian wight,
  Do homage to thy King;
And highly praise His humble pomp,
  Which He from Heaven doth bring.

FOR CHRISTMAS DAY.

[THIS Christmas Hymn is by Bishop Hall, equally celebrated as an eminent divine, and a satiric poet. He was a contemporary of Shakespeare, Jonson, Spenser, and the other stars of the Elizabethan age.]

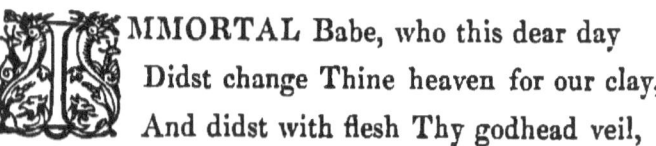MMORTAL Babe, who this dear day
Didst change Thine heaven for our clay,
And didst with flesh Thy godhead veil,
Eternal Son of God, all hail!

Thine, happy star, ye angels, sing
Glory on high to Heaven's King.
Run, shepherds, leave your nightly watch,
See heaven come down to Bethlehem's cratch.

Worship, ye sages of the east,
The King of God in meanness dressed.

O blessed maid, smile and adore
The God thy womb and arms have bore.

Star, angels, shepherds, and wild sages,
Thou virgin glory of all ages,
Restorèd frame of Heaven and Earth,
Joy in your dear Redeemer's birth!

THE SHEPHERDS' SONG.

[This Carol, or Hymn for Christmas, as it is termed in the original, was composed by Edmund Bolton: it is reprinted from *England's Helicon*, 1600.]

SWEET Music, sweeter far
    Than any song is sweet.
  Sweet music heavenly rare,
  Mine ears, O peers, doth greet.
You gentle flocks—whose fleeces, pearled with dew,
  Resemble Heaven, whom golden drops make
      bright—
Listen, O listen, now; O not to you
  Our pipes make sport to shorten weary night,
    But voices most divine
      Make blissful harmony—
    Voices that seem to shine;
      For what else clears the sky?

Tunes can we hear, but not the singers see;
The tune's divine, and so the singers be.

  Lo, how the firmament
   Within an azure fold
  The flock of stars hath pent,
   That we might them behold.
Yet from their beams proceedeth not this light,
 Nor can their crystals such reflection give.
What then doth make the element so bright?
 The heavens are come down upon earth to live.
  But hearken to the song,
   Glory to glory's King,
  And peace all men among,
   These choristers do sing.
Angels they are, as also Shepherds, He
Whom in our fear we do admire to see.

  " Let not amazement blind
   Your souls," said he, " annoy:
  To you and all mankind
   My message bringeth joy.
For lo, the world's great Shepherd now is born,
 A blessed babe, an Infant full of power:

After long night, up-risen is the morn,
  Renowning Bethlehem in the Saviour.
    Sprung is the perfect day,
      By prophets seen afar,
    Sprung is the perfect May,
      Which Winter cannot mar."
In David's city doth this Sun appear,
Clouded in flesh, yet Shepherds sit we here.

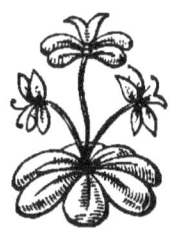

CHRISTMAS TIDE.

[THIS song of Shakespeare, although a mere scrap, breathes a delightful spirit of fancy blended with religious feeling. It is to be regretted that the poet of all time has only left us a few fragments relating to our subject.]

SOME say that ever 'gainst that season comes,
Wherein our Saviour's birth is celebrated,
The bird of dawning singeth all night long:
And then, they say, no spirit dares stir abroad;
The nights are wholesome; then no planets strike,
No fairy takes, nor witch hath power to charm,
So hallowed, and so gracious is the time.

HYMN ON THE NATIVITY OF MY SAVIOUR.

[THE following Carol, or Hymn, was written by Ben Jonson, about the year 1600.]

 SING the birth was born to night,
The author both of life and light;
The angel so did sound it,
And like the ravished shepherds said,
Who saw the light and were afraid,
Yet searched, and true they found it.

The Son of God th' Eternal King,
That did us all salvation bring,
And freed the soul from danger;
He whom the whole world could not take,
The word, which heaven and earth did make,
Was now laid in a manger.

The Father's wisdom willed it so,
The Son's obedience knew no No,
   Both wills were in one stature;
And as that wisdom had decreed,
The Word was now made Flesh indeed,
   And took on him our nature.

What comfort by Him do we win,
Who made Himself the Prince of sin,
   To make us heirs of Glory!
To see this babe all innocence,
A martyr born in our defence:
   Can man forget this story?

THE ANGELS' SONG.

[WILLIAM DRUMMOND, of Hawthornden, the friend of Ben Jonson, was the author of the two following sonnets. Jonson once trudged on foot to Scotland to see and converse with the man whom he had long known as a friendly correspondent. From Jonson's rude manners it does not appear that their mutual regard was enhanced.]

RUN, Shepherds, run where Bethlem blest
    appears,
    We bring the best of news, be not dismayed,
A Saviour there is born, more old than years
    Amidst Heaven's rolling heights this earth who
        stayed ;
    In a poor cottage inned, a Virgin Maid,
    There is He poorly swaddled, in manger laid,
A weakling did Him bear, who all upbears,
To whom too narrow swaddlings are our spheres :

Run, shepherds, run, and solemnize His birth,
  This is that night—no, day grown great with bliss,
  In which the power of Satan broken is;
In Heaven be glory, peace unto the Earth,
  Thus singing through the air the angels swam,
  And cope of stars re-echoèd the same.

CAROLS.

REMEMBER, O THOU MAN.

[This Christmas Carol is the last of the "Country Pastimes," in "Melismata: Musicall Phansies fitting the Court, Citie, and Country Humours," edited by Ravenscroft, 4to. 1611. It is paraphrased in "Ane compendious booke of Godly and Spirituall Songs ... with sundrie ... ballates changed out of prophaine Songes, &c.," printed by Andro Hart, in Edinburgh, 1621.

>   Remember, man, remember, man,
>   That I thy saull from Sathan wan,
>   And has done for thee what I can, &c.

It was formerly believed that this piece contained the original of *God save the King*.

Carols of this description, the writers of Elizabeth's reign denominated "Suffering Ballads."]

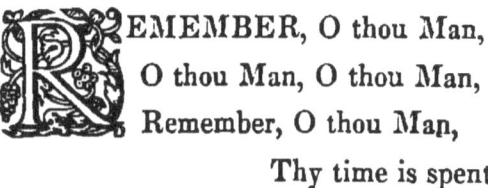EMEMBER, O thou Man,
O thou Man, O thou Man,
Remember, O thou Man,
   Thy time is spent.

Remember, O thou Man,
How thou camest to me then,
And I did what I can,
    Therefore repent.

Remember Adam's fall,
O thou Man, O thou Man,
Remember Adam's fall
    From Heaven to Hell.

Remember Adam's fall,
How we were condemned all
To Hell perpetual,
    There for to dwell.

Remember God's goodness,
O thou Man, O thou Man,
Remember God's goodness
    And promise made.

Remember God's goodness,
How he sent his Son, doubtless,
Our sins for to redress,
    Be not afraid.

The Angels all did sing,
O thou Man, O thou Man,
The Angels all did sing
  Upon the Shepherds' hill.

The Angels all did sing
Praises to our Heavenly King,
And peace to man living,
  With right good will.

The Shepherds amazed were,
O thou Man, O thou Man,
The Shepherds amazed were
  To hear the Angels sing.

The Shepherds amazed were
How this should come to pass,
That Christ our Messias
  Should be our King.

To Bethlehem did they go,
O thou Man, O thou Man,
To Bethlehem did they go,
  This thing to see.

To Bethlehem did they go,
To see whether it was so,
Whether Christ was born or no,
    To set us free.

As the Angels before did say,
O thou Man, O thou Man,
As the Angels before did say,
    So it came to pass.

As the Angels before did say,
They found him wrapt in hay
In a manger where he lay,
    So poor he was.

In Bethlehem he was born,
O thou Man, O thou Man,
In Bethlehem he was born
    For mankind dear.

In Bethlehem he was born
For us that were forlorn,
And therefore took no scorn
    Our sins to bear.

In a manger laid he was,
O thou Man, O thou Man,
In a manger laid he was
    At this time present.

In a manger laid he was
Between an ox and an ass,
And all for our trespass,
    Therefore repent.

Give thanks to God alway,
O thou Man, O thou Man,
Give thanks to God alway,
    With Hearts most joyfully:

Give thanks to God alway,
Upon this blessed day
Let all men sing and say
    Holy, Holy.

A CHRISTMAS CAROL.

[AMONG all our English poets, the one, who has left us by far the most complete contemporary picture of the Christmas season, was a country clergyman of the reign of Charles I. who held a small living in a remote part of Devonshire. This was Robert Herrick, the author of *Hesperides*, and of the following beautiful Carol.]

Chorus.

WHAT sweeter music can we bring
   Than a carol, for to sing
   The birth of this our Heavenly King?
Awake the voice! awake the string!
Heart, ear, and eye, and everything,
Awake! the while the active finger
Runs division with the singer.

I.

Dark and dull night, fly hence away,
And give the honor to this day,
That sees December turned to May.

II.

If we may ask the reason, say
The why, and wherefore all things here
Seem like the spring time of the year?

III.

Why does the chilling winter's morn
Smile, like a field beset with corn?
Or smell, like to a mead new shorn,
Thus, on the sudden?

IV.

Come and see
The cause, why things thus fragrant be:
'Tis He is born, whose quickening birth
Gives life and lustre, public mirth,
To Heaven and the under Earth.

Chorus.

We see Him come, and know Him ours,
Who with His sunshine and His showers,
Turns all the patient ground to flowers.

I.

The Darling of the world is come,
And fit it is we find a room
To welcome Him.

II.

The nobler part
Of all the house here, is the heart.

Chorus.

Which we will give Him; and bequeath
This holly and this ivy wreath,
To do Him honour who's our King,
And Lord of all this revelling.

CAROLS.

THE STAR SONG.

THE FLOURISH OF MUSICK; THEN FOLLOW THE SONG.

[THIS delightful Carol is by the author of the preceding. The concluding lines, with their allusion to wassailing, represent very well the spirit of the season in old times,—a mixture of devotion and thankfulness, with a little worldly, yet harmless, rejoicing.]

I.

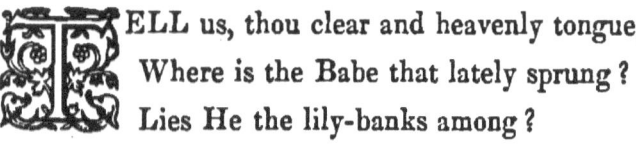ELL us, thou clear and heavenly tongue,
Where is the Babe that lately sprung?
Lies He the lily-banks among?

II.

Or say, if this new Birth of ours
Sleeps, laid within some ark of flowers,
Spangled with dew-light? thou canst clear
All doubts, and manifest the where.

III.

Declare to us, bright star, if we shall seek
Him in the morning's blushing cheek,
Or search the beds of spices through,
To find Him out?

Star.

No, this ye need not do;
But only come and see Him rest,
A Princely Babe, in's mother's breast.

Chorus.

He's seen! He's seen! why then around,
Let's kiss the sweet and holy ground;
And all rejoice that we have found
A King, before conception, crowned.

IV.

Come then, come then, and let us bring
Unto our pretty twelfth-tide King,
Each one his several offering.

Chorus.

And when night comes we'll give Him wassailing;
And that His treble honours may be seen,
We'll choose Him King, and make His mother queen.

AN ODE ON THE BIRTH OF OUR SAVIOUR.

[This also is from the pen of Herrick. The expression "scorn," in the fourth line, although sounding strangely to modern ears, is a term frequently to be met with in old popular literature. It occurs in *God rest you Merry Gentlemen*, and other Carols in this collection.]

IN numbers, and but these few,
I sing thy birth, Oh Jesu!
Thou pretty Baby, born here,
With sup'rabundant scorn here;
Who for Thy princely port here,
Hadst for Thy place
Of Birth, a base
Out-stable for thy court here.

Instead of neat inclosures
Of interwoven osiers;

Instead of fragrant posies,
Of daffodils, and roses;
Thy cradle, Kingly Stranger,
    As Gospel tells,
    Was nothing else
But, here, a homely manger.

But we with silks, not cruells,[1]
With sundry precious jewels,
And lily-work will dress Thee:
And as we dispossess Thee
Of clouds, we'll make a chamber,
    Sweet Babe, for Thee
    Of ivory,
And plastered round with amber.

The Jews, they did disdain Thee,
But we will entertain Thee
With glories to await here
Upon Thy princely state here;
And more for love than pity,
    From year to year
We'll make Thee, here
A free-born of our city.

[1] Worsteds.

CHRISTMAS DAY.

[GEORGE WITHER, the author of the following Carol, was both a poet and soldier in the time of the Civil Wars. In the former character, however, he is better known to posterity. His poems, of which he has left us several small volumes, are graceful and tender, and some of them are invariably included in all collections of old poetry. Mr. Russell Smith has recently reprinted, in a very handsome form, his *Hymns and Songs of the Church*.]

AS on the night before this happy morn,
    A blessed angel unto shepherds told,
    Where (in a stable) He was poorly born,
Whom nor the earth, nor heaven of heavens can
    hold:
Through Bethlem rung
    This news at their return:
Yea, angels sung
    That God with us was born;
And they made mirth because we should not mourn.

Their angel-carol sing we, then,
To God on high all glory be,
For peace on earth bestoweth He,
And showeth favor unto men.

This favor Christ vouchsafed for our sake ;
  To buy us thrones, He in a manger lay ;
Our weakness took, that we His strength might take ;
  And was disrobed that He might us array ;
    Our flesh He wore,
      Our sin to wear away ;
    Our curse He bore,
      That we escape it may ;
And wept for us, that we might sing for aye.

With angels, therefore, sing again,
To God on high all glory be ;
For peace on earth bestoweth He,
And showeth favor unto men.

THE VIRGIN MOTHER.

[THE popularity of the following Carol is the only excuse for its insertion here. The poetry is of the most poverty-stricken description,—and yet there is a quaint earnestness that now and then arrests the reader's attention. Hone inserts it in his list, and the Carol printers deem it sufficiently a favourite to reproduce it each Christmas.]

COME behold the Virgin Mother
    Fondly leaning on her child,
    Nature shows not such another,
Glorious, holy, meek and mild:
Bethlehem's ancient walls enclose him,
    Dwelling place of David once;
Now no friendly homestead knows him,
    Tho' the noblest of his sons.

Many a prophecy before him
    Publish'd his bright advent long,

Guardian Angels low adore him
  In a joyous heavenly song;
Eastern Sages see with wonder
  His bright Star illume the sky,
O'er the volumes old they ponder,
  Volumes of dark prophecy.

Royal Bethlehem how deserted,
  All his pomp and splendour lost;
Is a stable, vile and dirty,
  All the welcome you can boast?
Far they travel, oft enquiring
  Where the wondrous babe is born:
On they come with great desiring,
  Although others treat with scorn.

See, a babe of days and weakness
  Heaven's Almighty now appears,
Liable to death and sickness,
  Shame and agony and tears.
Sovereign he and great Creator,
  He who form'd the heav'ns and earth
Yet takes on him human nature,
  Angels wonder at his birth.

Why, ah, why this condescension,
    God with mortal man to dwell?
Why lay by his grand pretension,
    He who does all thrones excell?
'Tis to be a man, a brother,
    With us sinners of mankind:
Vain we search for such another,
    Ne'er we love like this shall find.

'Tis to make himself an offering
    As a pure atoning lamb,
Souls redeeming by his suffering,
    That in human flesh he came;
As a God he could not suffer,
    He a body true must have;
As a man what he might offer
    Could not satisfy or save.

Tho' an infant now you view him,
    He shall fill his Father's throne,
Gather all the Nations to him;
    Every knee shall then bow down:
Foes shall at his presence tremble,
    Great and small, and quick and dead,

None can fly, none dare dissemble,
   None find where to hide his head.

Friends! Oh then in cheerful voices
   They shall shout with glad acclaim,
While each rising saint rejoices,
   Saints of high or lowest fame.
Then what different appearing
   We 'mong mortal tribes shall find;
Groaning those who now are sneering,
   Triumphing the humble mind.

May we now, that day forestalling,
   Hear the word, and read and pray,
Listen to the Gospel calling,
   And with humble heart obey.
Give us hearty true repentance,
   Live in faith and holiness;
Then we need not fear thy sentence,
   But may trust thy saving grace,
        Hallelujah, Hallelujah, Hallelujah,
          Praise the Lord.

JOY TO THE WORLD.

[AMONGST all the jubilant Carols this is certainly the greatest favourite with the good people of Devon and Cornwall. The tune to which it is usually sung is very fine. The Carol may date back to the beginning of the last century, but it is probably more recent.]

JOY to the world, the Lord is come,
    Let earth receive her King;
  Let every tongue with sacred mirth
  His loud applauses sing.

Hark, hark, what news, what joyful news,
    To all the nations round;
To-day rejoice, a King is born,
    Who is with glory crown'd.

Behold! He comes, the tidings spread,
    A Saviour full of grace:
He comes, in mercy, to restore,
    A sinful, fallen race.

HARK! THE HERALD ANGELS SING.

[THIS Carol possesses none of the elements of the old legendary Carols, yet, as one of the oldest and most popular religious hymns, a place is accorded to it here. Each Christmas it is invariably presented to us, with other favourites, by the singers and chapmen.]

HARK! the herald Angels sing,
Glory to the new born King,
Peace on earth and mercy mild,
God and sinner reconcil'd.
    Hark! the herald Angels sing,
    Glory to the new born King.

Joyful all ye nations rise,
Join the triumph of the skies,
With the angelic host proclaim,
Christ is born in Bethlehem.
    Hark! the herald, &c.

Christ by highest Heaven ador'd,
Christ the everlasting Lord !
Late in time behold him come,
Offspring of a Virgin's womb.[1]
    Hark ! the herald, &c.

Hail the Heaven-born Prince of Peace !
Hail the Sun of Righteousness !
Light and life to all he brings,
Risen with healing in his wings.
    Hark ! the herald, &c.

Mild he lays his glory by,
Born that man no more may die,
Born to raise the sons of earth,
Born to give them second birth.
    Hark ! the herald, &c.

---

[1] A broadside copy, printed at Hayle, in Cornwall, gives another verse after this, but the lines appear to have been copied from some local Hymn-book :—

> Veil'd in Flesh the Godhead he,
> Hail th' incarnate Deity ;
> Pleas'd as man with man appear,
> Jesus our Immanuel here.

WHILST SHEPHERDS WATCH'D.

[This piece enjoys great popularity in the rural districts. In the West it is frequently to be met with in the local Hymn-books. It is probably not older than the last century.]

WHILST shepherds watch'd their flocks by night,
All seated on the ground,
The Angel of the Lord came down,
And glory shone around.

" Fear not," said he, for mighty dread
Had seized their troubled mind,
" Glad tidings of great joy I bring
To you and all mankind.

" To you in David's town this day
Is born of David's line
A Saviour, which is Christ the Lord;
And this shall be the sign,—

" The heavenly Babe you there shall find,
To human view display'd,
All meanly wrapped in swaddling bands,
And in a manger laid."

Thus spake the Seraph, and forthwith
Appeared a heavenly throng
Of Angels praising God, and thus
Address'd their joyful song :—

" All glory be to God on high,
And to the earth be peace,
Good-will henceforth from Heav'n to men,
Begin and never cease. Hallelujah."

HARK! ALL AROUND THE WELKIN RINGS.

[THE use of the old Saxon word *welkin*, for heaven, or the sky, indicates the probable age of this piece. The term was occasionally used in poetry as late as the reign of Queen Anne.]

HARK! all around the welkin rings,
    Bright Seraphs hail the morn,
  That ushers in the King of Kings,
    That saw a Saviour born.

Chorus.

Ye people on earth, your voices now raise,
To Christ our Redeemer, in carols of praise,
Hallelujah! praise the Lord, hallelujah!

Then shining heralds from on high
    Those joyful tidings bear,
With acclamations down the sky,
    And humble shepherds hear.

" Glory to God, and peace to men,"
    The heavenly choir did sing;
Let earth repeat the sound again,
    And hail the new-born King.

This is the day our Lord did choose
    To visit mortal man;
And from the bands of sin to loose
    All those that trust in him.

Lord Jesus, let thy kingdom spread
    Through all the earth below;
Let every land thy wonders read,
    And thy salvation know.

Hosanna! let all the earth and heaven
    Salute the happy morn;
To-day the promis'd child is given,
    And God himself is born.

MORTALS, AWAKE, WITH ANGELS JOIN.

[ALTHOUGH this Carol is included in most of the broadside sheets of the present day, still it is doubtful if it was composed later than the time of Watt or Wesley.]

MORTALS, awake, with angels join,
    And chant the solemn lay;
    Joy, love, and gratitude, combine
To hail th' auspicious day.

In heaven the rapturous song began,
    And sweet seraphic fire
Thro' all the shining legions ran,
    And strung and tun'd the lyre.

Swift thro' the vast expanse it flew,
    And loud the echo roll'd;
The theme, the song, the joy was new,
    'Twas more than heaven could hold.

Down thro' the portals of the sky
　　Th' impetuous torrent ran;
And angels flew with eager joy
　　To bear the news to man.

[Wrapt in the silence of the night
　　Lay all the Eastern world,
When bursting, glorious, heavenly light
　　The wondrous scene unfurl'd.]

Hark! the cherubic armies shout,
　　And glory leads the song;
Good-will and peace are heard throughout
　　Th' harmonious heavenly throng.

O for a glance of heavenly love
　　Our hearts and songs to raise,
Sweetly to bear our souls above,
　　And mingle with their lays!

With joy the chorus we'll repeat,
　　" Glory to God on high!
Good-will and peace are now complete;
　　Jesus was born to die."

Hail, Prince of Life! for ever hail!
  Redeemer, brother, friend!
Tho' earth, and time, and life should fail
  Thy praise shall never end.

A NEW CHRISTMAS CAROL.

[Such is the title of a pleasing little hymn which occurs on a sheet printed at the beginning of the present century. It does not appear to have been gathered into any previous collection.]

IT is the day, the Holy day,
    On which our Lord was born,
    And sweetly doth the sunbeams gild
The dew besprinkled thorn.
The birds sing thro' the heavens,
    And the breezes gently play,
And song and sunshine lovely,
    Begins this Holy day.

'Twas in a humble manger,
    A little lowly shed,
With cattle at his infant feet,
    And shepherds at his head,

The Saviour of this sinful world,
  In innocence first lay,
While Wise Men made their offerings
  To him this Holy day.

He comes to save the perishing,
  To waft the sighs to heaven
Of guilty men, who truly sought
  To weep, to be forgiven.
And intercessor still he shines,
  And men to him should pray
At His altar's feet for meekness
  Upon this Holy day.

As flowers still bloom fair again,
  Though all their life seems shed,
Thus we shall rise with life once more,
  Tho' number'd with the dead.
Then may our stations be near Him,
  To whom we worship pay,
And praise with heart felt gratitude,
  Upon this Holy day.

CHRIST WAS BORN ON CHRISTMAS DAY.

[This is another of the Macaronic Carols, and will be found to be one of the most jubilant and spirited in our collection. It is believed to be of Swedish origin, possessing the true choral resonance of the Scandinavian Ballad. We are indebted to the Rev. J. M. Neale for this English version.]

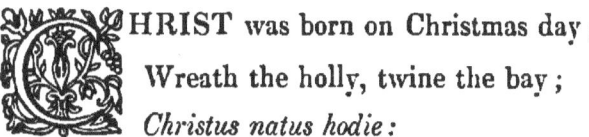HRIST was born on Christmas day;
Wreath the holly, twine the bay;
Christus natus hodie:
The Babe, the Son, the Holy One of Mary.

He is born to set us free,
He is born our Lord to be,
Ex Mariâ Virgine:
The God, the Lord, by all adored for ever.

K

Let the bright red berries glow
Every-where in goodly show;
Christus natus hodie:
The Babe, the Son, the Holy One of Mary.

Christian men, rejoice and sing;
'Tis the birthday of a King,
Ex Mariâ Virgine:
The God, the Lord, by all adored for ever.

Night of sadness;
Morn of gladness ever-more: ever, ever,
After many troubles sore,
Morn of gladness, ever-more, and ever-more.

Midnight scarcely pass'd and over,
Drawing to this holy morn,
Very early, very early
Christ was born.

Sing out with bliss,
His name is this; Emmanuel:
As 'twas foretold, in days of old,
By Gabriel.

Midnight scarcely pass'd and over,
Drawing to this holy morn;
Very early, very early
Christ was born.

Part III.

NUMERAL CAROLS.

THE SEVEN JOYS.

[NUMERAL Hymns were common in the olden time. Frequently they were set as tasks for children to acquire, and he received most praise who could ascend correctly to the highest number.

The following is one of the commonest, at the same time that it is one of the most ancient, of all our popular Carols. The original, preserved among the Sloane MSS., and of a date not later than the fourteenth century, is entitled " *Joyes Fyve.*" As a specimen I give the first verse.

> Ye ferste joye as i zu telle
> W*t* mary met seynt Gab'elle,
> Heyl mary i grete ye welle,
>   w*t* fad*r* & sone & holy gost.

Perhaps some apology is necessary for the expression which is made to rhyme with " one " in the first verse. Another word was not easily found, and the taste of the time was widely different from what it is now. At first I was inclined to omit the Carol, but its popularity pleaded its insertion.]

CAROLS.

THE first good joy our Mary had,
It was the joy of one,
To see her own Son Jesus
To suck at her breast bone;
To suck at her breast bone,
Good man, and blessed may he be
Both Father, Son, and Holy Ghost,
And Christ to eternity.

The next good joy our Mary had,
It was the joy of two,
To see her own Son Jesus
To make the lame to go;
To make the lame to go,
Good man, &c.

The next good joy our Mary had,
It was the joy of three;
To see her own Son Jesus
To make the blind to see;
To make the blind to see,
Good man, &c.

The next good joy our Mary had,
    It was the joy of four,
To see her own Son Jesus
    To read the Bible o'er;
To read the Bible o'er,
        Good man, &c.

The next good joy our Mary had,
    It was the joy of five,
To see her own Son Jesus
    To raise the dead alive;
To raise the dead alive,
        Good man, &c.

The next good joy our Mary had,
    It was the joy of six,
To see her own Son Jesus
    To wear the crucifix;
To wear the crucifix,
        Good man, &c.

The next good joy our Mary had,
    Is was the joy of seven,

To see her own Son Jesus
  To wear the crown of Heaven;
To wear the crown of Heaven,
    Good man, and blessed may he be,
    Both Father, Son, and Holy Ghost,
    And Christ to eternity.

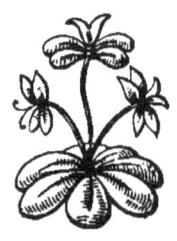

A NEW DIAL.

[COPIED from a leaf of an old Almanack preserved in the Bagford collection in the British Museum. The corresponding leaf is in the Black Letter, and bears the date 1625. The burden of this Carol is similar to that of one more modern, called "Man's Duty," given further on.]

1 NE God, one Baptism, and one Faith,
   One Truth there is, the Scripture saith.

2 Two Testaments (the Old and New)
   We do acknowledge to be true.

3 Three persons are in Trinity,
   Which make One God in Unity.

4 Four sweet Evangelists there are,
   Christ's birth, life, death, which do declare.

5 Five Senses, (like Five Kings) maintain
   In every Man a several reign.

6 Six days to labour, is not wrong,
   For God himself did work so long.

7 Seven Liberal Arts hath God sent down,
   With Divine skill Man's Soul to crown.

8 Eight in Noah's Ark alive were found,
   When (in a word) the World lay drowned.

9 Nine Muses (like the heaven's Nine Spheres)
   With sacred Tunes entice our ears.

10 Ten Statutes God to Moses gave,
   Which kept or broke, do spill or save.

11 Eleven with Christ in Heaven do dwell,
   The Twelfth for ever burns in Hell.

12 Twelve are attending on God's Son,
   Twelve make our Creed. The Dial's done.

   Count one the first hour of thy Birth,
   The hours that follow, lead to Earth;
   Count Twelve, thy doleful striking knell,
   And then thy Dial shall go well.

MAN'S DUTY;

OR, MEDITATION FOR THE TWELVE HOURS OF THE DAY.

[THE following Carol is selected as a specimen from several others. It will remind the reader of the well-known German Watchman's Song, which I am satisfied would be a great favourite with the peasantry if it once got into the hawkers' broad-sheets.]

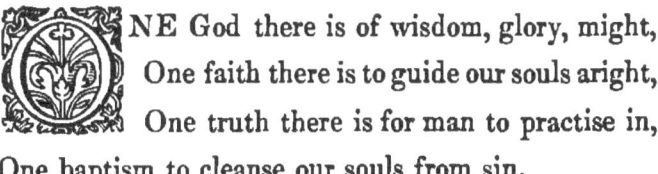NE God there is of wisdom, glory, might,
One faith there is to guide our souls aright,
One truth there is for man to practise in,
One baptism to cleanse our souls from sin.

Two Testaments there are, the Old and New,
In which the Law and Gospel thou may'st view;
The one for works and deeds doth precepts give,
The other saith the just by faith shall live.

Three persons in the glorious Trinity
Make one true God in perfect unity,
The Father, Son, and Holy Ghost, those three
For ever equal and eternal be.

Four most divine and righteous holy men
They did the life of our Redeemer pen,
They were Mathew, Mark, and Luke, and John
    likewise,
Whose righteous truth let every Christian prize.

Five senses do in every man maintain
A governing power, rule and reign ;
The hearing, seeing, tasting, feeling, smelling,
Which at thy death will leave thee and thy dwelling.

Six days, O man, thou hast to labour in,
So merciful and good thy God hath been,
Of seven unto himself he took but one,
O rob him not of that to leave him none.

Seven liberal arts, by a divine decree,
Unto man's knowing soul united be
Rhetoric, grammar, music and geometry,
Arithmetic, logic, and astronomy.

Eight persons in the ark of Noah were
When God he would the world no longer spare;
Sin did abound, therefore all flesh he drown'd
Which in that ship of safety were not bound.

Nine Muses their harmonious voices raise
To sing our blessed dear Redeemer's praise,
Who is the spring from whence all blessings flow
To us poor living mortals here below.

There are commandments ten we should obey,
And yet how apt we are to go astray,
Leaving them all our folly to pursue,
As if we did not care what God could do.

Eleven disciples did with Jesus pray
When Judas did our Saviour Christ betray,
Though, covetous for greedy gain, he fell
To be perdition's child condemned to hell.

Twelve tribes there were amongst our fathers old,
Twelve articles our Christian faith does hold,
Twelve gates in New Jerusalem there be,
Unto which city Christ bring you and me.

Part IV.

CAROLS IN PRAISE OF THE HOLLY AND IVY.

HOLLY AND IVY MADE A GREAT PARTY.

[THE custom of decking houses and churches with evergreens, towards the close of the year, appears to be of very ancient date; it being, in fact, one of those remnants of Paganism, which, although forbidden by the councils of the early Christian Church, had obtained too strong a hold on the prejudices of the people to be readily relinquished, as its transmission down to the present day serves to prove.

I am indebted to Mr. Wright's MS. for the following.]

OLLY and Ivy made a great party,
Who should have the mastery
  In lands where they go.

Then spake Holly, " I am fierce and jolly,
I will have the mastery
  In lands where we go."

Then spake Ivy, " I am loud and proud,
And I will have the mastery
        In lands where we go."

Then spake Holly, and bent him down on his knee,
" I pray thee, gentle Ivy,
Essay me no villany
        In lands where we go."

HERE COMES HOLLY.

[This ancient piece is taken from Mr. Wright's early volume of Carols. The spelling has been a little modernised.]

ERE comes Holly, that is so gent,[1]
To please all men is his intent.
        Alleluia !

But Lord and Lady of this hall,
Whosoever against Holly call.
        Alleluia !

Whosoever against Holly doth cry,
In a lepe[2] he shall hang full high.
        Alleluia !

Whosoever against Holly doth sing,
He may weep, and his hands wring.
        Alleluia !

[1] Gallant, courteous.   [2] A large fruit basket.

NAY, IVY, NAY!

[THIS quaint Carol is of the time of Henry VI. Stow says, " every man's house of olde time was decked with Holly and Ivie in the winter, especially at Christmas." It appears that formerly it was the custom at this season to set up in each village a long pole, decked with Holly and Ivy, after the fashion of the May-pole in summer time.

From the Stationer's books we learn that W. Copland paid 4d. for a licence from the company, to print " A ballette entitled *holy and hyve.*"]

AY, Ivy, nay, it shall not be, I wis,
Let Holly have the mastery as the manner is.

Holly standeth in the hall fair to behold,
Ivy stands without the door ; she is full sore a cold.
Nay, Ivy, nay, &c.

Holly and his merry men, they dance now and they sing ;
Ivy and her maidens, they weep, and their hands wring.
Nay, Ivy, nay, &c.

Ivy hath a lybe,[1] she caught it with the cold,
So may they all have, that do with Ivy hold.
    Nay, Ivy, nay, &c.

Holly he hath berries, as red as any rose,
The foresters, the hunters, keep them from the does.
    Nay, Ivy, nay, &c.

Ivy she hath berries as black as any sloe,
There come the owls and eat them as they go.
    Nay, Ivy, nay, &c.

Holly he hath birds a full fair flock,
The nightingale, the poppinjay, the gentle laverock.
    Nay, Ivy, nay, &c.

Good Ivy, say to us, what birds hast thou,
None but the owlet that cries How! How!
    Nay, Ivy, nay, &c.

[1] This word is not explained by any glossary.

HOLLY CAROL.

[WE are indebted to Shakespeare's pen for this pleasing little piece.]

BLOW, blow, thou winter wind,
    Thou art not so unkind
        As man's ingratitude;
Thy tooth is not so keen,
Because thou art not seen,
    Although thy breath be rude.
Heigh, ho! sing heigh, ho! unto the green holly:
Most friendship is feigning, most loving mere folly;
    Then, heigh, ho! the holly!
    This life is most jolly.

Freeze, freeze, thou bitter sky,
Thou dost not bite so nigh
    As benefits forgot:

Though thou the waters warp,
　　　　Thy sting is not so sharp
　　　　　　As friend remembered not.
Heigh, ho! sing heigh, ho! unto the green holly:
Most friendship is feigning, most loving mere folly;
　　　　　Then, heigh, ho! the holly!
　　　　　This life is most jolly.

THE HOLLY AND THE IVY.

[AN old broadside, printed a century and a half since, supplies the following. It does not appear to have been included in a collection before. The curious similes betwixt the holly and certain events in the life of Christ may yet be occasionally heard in the discourse of aged people. The Holly, from time immemorial, has been looked upon as a favoured evergreen, typical of the mission of Our Saviour.]

HE holly and the ivy
    Now are both well grown,
    Of all the trees that are in the wood
    The holly bears the crown.

Chorus.

The rising of the sun,
    The running of the deer,
The playing of the merry organ,
    The singing in the choir.

The holly bears a blossom
  As white as the lily flower,
And Mary bore sweet Jesus Christ
  To be our sweet Saviour.

The holly bears a berry
  As red as any blood,
And Mary bore sweet Jesus Christ
  To do poor sinners good.

The holly bears a prickle
  As sharp as any thorn,
And Mary bore sweet Jesus Christ
  On Christmas day in the morn.

The holly bears a bark
  As bitter as any gall,
And Mary bore sweet Jesus Christ
  For to reedem us all.

The holly and the ivy
  Now are both well grown,
Of all the trees that are in the wood
  The holly bears the crown.

Part V.

CAROLS IN PRAISE OF THE BOAR'S HEAD.

TIDINGS I BRING YOU FOR TO TELL.

[UNDER the head of Boar's Head Carols I have grouped together a few that were formerly in much request at Christmas celebrations. In those days Carols of this kind usually heralded the entertainment of good things provided by the generous host.

The first dish that was served up in the old baronial halls was the Boar's Head, which was brought in with great state, and with minstrelsy. Between the flourishes of the heralds' trumpets, Carols were chanted forth. The one which immediately follows is taken from Mr. T. Wright's MS., the spelling being modernised.]

TIDINGS I bring you for to tell
What in wild forest me befell,
When I in with a wild beast fell,
With a boar so bryme.[1]

[1] Fierce.

A boar so bryme that me pursued,
Me for to kill so sharply moved,
That brymly beast so cruel and rude,
　　　There tamed I him,
And reft from him both life and limb.

Truly, to show you this is true,
His head I with my sword did hew,
To make this day new mirth for you
　　　Now eat thereof anon.

Eat, and much good do it you ;
Take you bread and mustard thereto.
Joy with me that this I have done,
I pray you be glad every one,
　　　And all rejoice as one.

THE BOAR'S HEAD IN HAND I BRING.

[THE following is, perhaps, the most ancient of all the Boar's Head Carols. It is preserved in a manuscript of the fifteenth century. It has been remarked, that, in spite of the invitations contained in these Carols to partake of the "first mess," the Boar's Head, it is conjectured, was little else but a show dish; for, in all the allusions to it, mention is only made of one head being served at each feast, though, even were the number greater, it could hardly have been sufficient to have yielded a mouthful a-piece to the numerous guests who were generally present at these entertainments. Between the courses the minstrels played and sang, the jesters cracked their smartest jokes, and practised their most extravagant antics; and I dare say, the famous Dance of Fools was not unfrequently performed at this particular juncture, before the attention of the guests came to be directed to the more exciting business which was so soon to follow.]

EY! Hey! Hey! Hey!
The Boar's head is armèd gay.

  The boar's head in hand I bring
  With garlands gay encircling,[1]

[1] *Porttorying* in the original,—a word not explained in any glossary.

I pray you all with me to sing,
           With Hey!

Lords, knights, and squires,
Parsons, priests, and vicars,
The boar's head is the first mess,[2]
           With Hey!

The boar's head, as I now say,
Takes its leave and goes away,
Goeth after the Twelfth day,
           With Hey!

Then comes in the second course with great pride,
The cranes, the herons, the bitterns, by their side,
The partridges, the plovers, the woodcocks, and the snipe,
Larks in hot snow, for the ladies to pick,
Good drink also, luscious and fine,
Blood of Allemaine, romnay, and wine,
           With Hey!

Good brewed ale and wine, I dare well say,
The boar's head with mustard armed so gay,

---

[2] That is, "the first dish."

Furmity for pottage, and venison fine,
And the umbles of the doe and all that ever comes in,
Capons well baked, with knuckles of the roe,
Raisins and currants, and other spices too,
    With Hey!

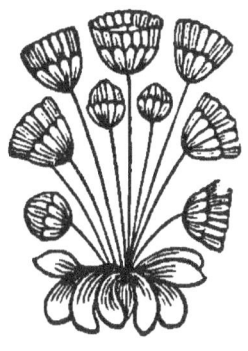

THE BOAR'S HEAD IN HAND BRING I.

[This Carol is taken from a single leaf, all that has been preserved, of a book of Carols printed by Wynkin de Worde in 1521. It is there entitled, "A Carol, brynging in the Bore's Head." This antique ceremony was observed up to a very recent period in Queen's College, Oxford, but with this considerable improvement indeed, that the Boar's head was neatly carved in wood.]

Caput Apri defero
Reddens laudes Domino.

THE boar's head in hand bring I,
With garlands gay and rosemary;
I pray you all sing merrily,
    Qui estis in convivio.

The boar's head, I understand,
Is the chief service in this land;
Look wherever it be found,
    Servite cum cantico.

Be glad, lords, both more or less,
    For this hath ordained our steward
To cheer you all this Christmas,
    The boar's head with mustard.[1]

---

[1] The imprint on the leaf which has preserved us this Carol is :—" Thus endeth the Christmasse Carroles, newely enprinted at Londo. in fletestrete at the sygne of the sonne by Wynkin de Worde. The yere of our lorde, M.D.XXI."

THE BOAR'S HEAD THAT WE BRING HERE.

[THIS Carol was first printed by Ritson from an ancient MS. in his possession, now deposited in the British Museum. The composition in all probability is of the reign of Henry VIII. As before stated, Nowel, or Noel, is the old French name for Christmas, and was the usual burden for Carols of this kind.]

OEL, Noel, Noel, Noel,
Tidings good I think to tell.

The boar's head, that we bring here,
Betokenth a prince without peer
Is born to-day to buy us dear,
    Noel.

The boar he is a sovereign beast,
And acceptable at every feast;
So might this lord be to greatest and least;
        Noel.

This boar's head we bring with song,
In worship of Him that thus sprung
From a virgin to redress all wrong;
        Noel.

THE BOAR IS DEAD.

[THIS Carol is the Christmas grace sung before Prince Henry, at St. John's College, Oxford, in 1607. The second verse would appear to give countenance to the pagan origin of our Christmas observances. The mention of Meleager in the first verse refers to the hero who slaughtered the famous old Calydonian Boar.]

HE Boar is dead,
   Lo, here is his head:
      What man could have done more
Than his head off to strike,
Meleager like,
   And bring it as I do before?

   He living spoiled
   Where good men toiled,
      Which made kind Ceres sorry;

But now, dead and drawn,
Is very good brawn,
    And we have brought it for ye.

Then set down the swineyard,
The foe to the vineyard,
    Let Bacchus crown his fall;
Let this boar's head and mustard
Stand for pig, goose, and custard,
    And so you are welcome all.

Part VI.

FESTIVE CAROLS.

ANGLO-NORMAN CAROL.

[This Carol, we are informed by the antiquaries, is the earliest known to have been written in our island. The thirteenth century is believed to be the period of its composition. The original is in the Anglo-Norman language. Some years ago it was discovered on a blank leaf in the middle of one of the manuscripts in the British Museum. The editor of *Christmas with the Poets* supposes this Carol to have been one of those in use among the bands of professional minstrels—half vagrants, half troubadours—who wandered from one to the other of the different castles of the Norman nobility, "discoursing sweet sounds" for the gratification of the assembled guests, and who were certain of a ready welcome on so festive an occasion as the celebration of the Christmas feast. The late Mr. Douce made an English version, inserted in *Brand's Antiquities;* but the following, from the pen of the editor previously alluded to, is preferred.]

LORDINGS, listen to our lay—
We have come from far away
   To seek Christmas;

In this mansion we are told
He his yearly feast doth hold:
    'T is to-day!
May joy come from God above,
To all those who Christmas love!

Lordings, I now tell you true,
Christmas bringeth unto you
    Only mirth;
His house he fills with many a dish
Of bread and meat and also fish,
    To grace the day.
May joy come from God above,
To all those who Christmas love!

Lordings, through our army's band
They say—who spends with open hand
    Free and fast,
And oft regales his many friends,
God gives him double what he spends,
    To grace the day.
May joy come from God above,
To all those who Christmas love!

Lordings, wicked men eschew,
In them never shall you view
    Aught that is good;
Cowards are the rabble rout,
Kick and beat the grumblers out,
    To grace the day.
May joys come from God above,
To all those who Christmas love.

To English Ale and Gascon wine,
And French, doth Christmas much incline—
    And Anjou's, too;
He makes his neighbour freely drink,
So that in sleep his head doth sink
    Often by day.
May joys flow from God above,
To all those who Christmas love.

Lords, by Christmas and the host
Of this mansion hear my toast—
    Drink it well—
Each must drain his cup of wine,
And I the first will toss off mine:
    Thus I advise.

Here then I bid you all *Wassail*,
Cursed be he who will not say, *Drinkhail*.[1]

---

[1] *Wassail* and *Drinkhail* are both derived from the Anglo-Saxon. They were the common drinking pledges of the age. *Wassail* is equivalent to the phrase " Your health," of the present day. *Drinkhail*, which literally signifies " drink health," was the usual acknowledgment of the other pledge.

SIR CHRISTMAS.

[AN ancient MS. in the British Museum furnishes the following Carol, which, in olden times, would appear to have been the initiatory welcome to the festivities of the season. The religious allusions, intermixed with invitations to partake of the good things of this life, mark the age of hearty hospitality and honest enjoyment,—before Puritanism came into fashion.]

OEL, Noel, Noel, Noel,
    Who is there, that singeth so, Noel,
        Noel, Noel?

I am here, Sir Christmas,
Welcome, my lord Sir Christmas,
Welcome to all both more or less;[1]
    Come near Noel.

[1] Great and small.

God be with you, Sir, tidings I you bring,
A maid hath born a Child full young,
The which causeth me to sing,
            Noel.

Christ is now born of a pure maid,
In an ox stall He is laid,
Wherefore sing we all at abraid,[2]
            Noel.

Drink you all right heartily,
Make good cheer and be right merry,
And sing with us now joyfully,
            Noel.

[2] Suddenly, or loudly.

A CAROL IN PRAISE OF ALE.

[IT has been remarked that during the continuance of the Christmas banquet there is no doubt but that various Carols were sung, either by the assembled company, or by the attendant minstrels, having, for their subject-matter, neither reference to the religious origin of the festival, nor to any of the particular ceremonies connected with it. The following drinking-song was probably of the number. It occurs in a MS. of the sixteenth century, in the British Museum, and is there entitled " A Christenmasse Carroll."]

BONE, God wot!
Sticks in my throat—
Without I have a draught
Of cornie ale,
Nappy and stale,
My life lies in great waste.
Some ale or beer,
Gentle butler,
Some liquor thou us show,

Such as you mash
Our throats to wash,
The best were that you brew.

Saint, master, and knight,
That Saint Malt hight,
Were pressed between two stones;
The sweet humour
Of his liquor
Would make us sing at once.
Master Wortley,
I dare well say,
I tell you as I think,
Would not, I say,
Bid us this day,
But that we should have drink.

His men so tall
Walk up his hall,
With many a comely dish;
Of his good meat
I cannot eat,
Without I drink, I wis.
Now give us drink,
And let cat wink,

I tell you all at once,
   It sticks so sore,
   I may sing no more,
Till I have drunken once.

A CAROL FOR A WASSAIL BOWL.

[THE following Carol was copied by Ritson from a scarce black-letter volume, in the Ashmolean Museum. The Boar's head and the Wassail bowl were the two most important accessories to Christmas in the olden time, and many are the allusions to the latter in our early English poets. The phrase "Wassail" occurs in the oldest Carol that has been handed down to us. New Year's eve and Twelfth-night were the occasions on which the Wassail bowl was chiefly in requisition. In the royal household of Henry VII., on Twelfth-night, the steward was enjoined, when he entered with the spiced and smoking beverage, to cry "Wassail" three times, to which the royal chaplain had to answer with a Carol or song.]

 JOLLY Wassail Bowl,
A Wassail of good ale,
Well fare the butler's soul,
That setteth this to sale—
Our jolly Wassail.

Good dame, here at your door,
 Our Wassail we begin,
We are all maidens poor,
 We now pray let us in,
   With our Wassail.

Our Wassail we do fill
 With apples and with spice,
Then grant us your good will,
 To taste here once or twice
   Of our Wassail.

If any maidens be
 Here dwelling in this house,
They kindly will agree
 To take a full carouse
   Of our Wassail.

But here they let us stand
 All freezing in the cold;
Good master, give command
 To enter and be bold,
   With our Wassail.

Much joy into this hall
    With us is entered in,
Our master first of all,
    We hope will now begin,
            Of our Wassail.

And after, his good wife
    Our spiced bowl will try,—
The Lord prolong your life!
    Good fortune we espy,
            For our Wassail.

Some bounty from your hands,
    Our Wassail to maintain:
We'll buy no house nor lands
    With that which we do gain,
            With our Wassail.

This is our merry night
    Of choosing King and Queen,
Then be it your delight
    That something may be seen
            In our Wassail.

It is a noble part
  To bear a liberal mind;
God bless our master's heart!
  For here we comfort find,
        With our Wassail.

And now we must be gone,
  To seek out more good cheer;
Where bounty will be shown,
  As we have found it here,
        With our Wassail.

Much joy betide them all,
  Our prayers shall be still,
We hope, and ever shall,
  For this your great good will,
        To our Wassail.

GOD BLESS THE MASTER OF THIS HOUSE.

[RITSON, in his *Ancient Songs and Ballads*, gives the following simple little Carol as of the time of James I. See " The Wassailers' Carol " further on.]

GOD bless the master of this house,
    The mistress, also,
  And all the little children,
    That round the table go:

And all your kin and kinsfolk,
    That dwell both far and near;
I wish you a merry Christmas,
    And a happy new year.

CAROLS.

COME BRING WITH A NOISE.

[WE are indebted to the poet Herrick for the following Carol, descriptive of the ceremony attending the bringing in the Christmas or Yule log, a custom of very ancient date; yet, nevertheless, this is the first occasion that I find allusion to it in the writings of our earlier poets. The practice of burning a block, or faggot, at the Christmas season is still common in many parts of England. The eve before Christmas Day is the favourite time, when friendly neighbours surround the hearth, and Carols are sung.]

COME bring with a noise,
    My merry, merry boys,
    The Christmas log to the firing;
While my good dame, she
Bids ye all be free,
And drink to your heart's desiring.

With the last year's brand
Light the new block, and
For good success in his spending,

On your psalteries play,
That sweet luck may
Come while the log is a tending.

Drink now the strong beer,
Cut the white loaf here,
The while the meat is a shredding,
For the rare mince-pie,
And the plums stand by,
To fill the paste that's a kneading.

THE WASSAIL.

[HERRICK is the author of the following. As was stated in the introductory note to a Carol given in the first part of this little volume, *Wassail* is the ancient term for " your health," or " may you be in health." The custom of wishing prosperity to the owner of the house is yet common in many places. The " Waits " generally leave their benediction before going to another spot, and so do the poor little shivering carolists who wait at our door on the Holy morn, notwithstanding that the pious wish is contained in their usually concluding Carol, " God rest you Merry Gentlemen." The Puritans delayed the friendly task until New Year's Day,—a custom still followed in the villages of New England, whither it was carried by the Puritan Fathers.]

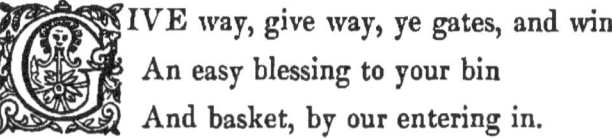IVE way, give way, ye gates, and win
An easy blessing to your bin
And basket, by our entering in.

May both with manchet[1] stand replete,
Your larder, too, so hung with meat,
That though a thousand thousand eat,

---

[1] Fine wheaten bread.

Yet, ere twelve moons shall whirl about
Their silv'ry spheres, there's none may doubt
But more's sent in than was served out.

Next, may your dairies prosper so,
As that your pans no ebb may know;
But if they do, the more to flow:

Like to a solemn sober stream,
Banked all with lilies, and the cream
Of sweetest cowslips filling them.

Then may your plants be pressed with fruit,
Nor bee nor hive you have be mute,
But sweetly sounding like a lute.

Next, may your duck and teeming hen,
Both to the cock's tread say, amen;
And for their two eggs render ten.

Last, may your harrows, shares, and ploughs,
Your stacks, your stocks, your sweetest mows,
All prosper by your virgin-vows.

Alas! we bless, but see none here,
That brings us either ale or beer;
In a dry house all things are near.

Let's leave a longer time to wait,
Where rust and cobwebs bind the gate,
And all live here with needy fate;

Where chimneys do for ever weep
For want of warmth, and stomachs keep
With noise the servants' eyes from sleep.

It is in vain to sing, or stay
Our free feet here, but we'll away,
Yet to the Larès this we'll say:

" The time will come, when you'll be sad,
And reckon this for fortune bad,
T' have lost the good ye might have had."

MERRY CHRISTMAS.

[WE are indebted to the poet Wither for the following lively verses on Christmas. They were penned some time before he joined the Puritan party. As has been stated, they introduce us to an amusing picture of the rejoicings of the season, ere the civil troubles of the reign of Charles I. had interfered to throw a damper on the national hilarity. The holly and the ivy had not yet come to be regarded as emblems of paganism. The Christmas log still blazed on the hospitable hearth, and music and dancing were far from being considered irrelevant amusements. The wassail bowl, too, was in fashion, and even mumming was indulged in by both young men and maidens—

"With twenty other gambols mo,
Because they would be merry."]

O, now is come our joyful'st feast;
   Let every man be jolly;
Each room with ivy leaves is drest,
   And every post with holly.

Though some churls at our mirth repine,
Round your foreheads garlands twine;
Drown sorrow in a cup of wine,
    And let us all be merry.

Now all our neighbours' chimneys smoke,
    And Christmas blocks are burning;
Their ovens they with baked meats choke,
    And all their spits are turning.
Without the door let sorrow lie;
And if for cold it hap to die,
We'll bury't in a Christmas pie,
    And evermore be merry.

Now every lad is wondrous trim,
    And no man minds his labour,
Our lasses have provided them
    A bag-pipe and a tabour;
Young men and maids, and girls and boys,
Give life to one another's joys;
And you anon shall by their noise
    Perceive that they are merry.

Rank misers now do sparing shun;
    Their hall of music soundeth;

And dogs thence with whole shoulders run,
    So all things there aboundeth.
The country folks themselves advance
With crowdy-muttons[1] out of France;
And Jack shall pipe, and Jill shall dance,
    And all the town be merry.

Ned Squash hath fetched his bands from pawn,
    And all his best apparel;
Brisk Nell hath bought a ruff of lawn
    With droppings of the barrel;
And those that hardly all the year
Had bread to eat, or rags to wear,
Will have both clothes and dainty fare,
    And all the day be merry.

Now poor men to the justices
    With capons make their errants;[2]
And if they hap to fail of these,
    They plague them with their warrants;

---

[1] Fiddlers.

[2] Formerly this was a custom on the part of tenants to their landlords, which came to be followed by all the poorer sort, who made their annual offering at the great man's shrine at this particular season of the year.

But now they feed them with good cheer,
And what they want they take in beer;
For Christmas comes but once a year,
   And then they shall be merry.

Good farmers in the country nurse
   The poor, that else were undone;
Some landlords spend their money worse,
   On lust and pride at London.
There the roysters they do play,
Drab and dice their lands away,
Which may be ours another day;
   And therefore let's be merry.

The client now his suit forbears,
   The prisoner's heart is eased;
The debtor drinks away his cares,
   And for the time is pleased.
Though other purses be more fat,
Why should we pine or grieve at that?
Hang sorrow! care will kill a cat,
   And therefore let's be merry.

Hark! how the wags abroad do call
   Each other forth to rambling:

Anon you'll see them in the hall
    For nuts and apples scrambling.
Hark! how the roofs with laughter sound!
Anon they'll think the house goes round;
For they the cellar's depth have found,
    And there they will be merry.

The wenches with their wassail bowls
    About the streets are singing;
The boys are come to catch the owls,
    The wild mare in is bringing.
Our kitchen-boy hath broke his box,[1]
And to the dealing of the ox
Our honest neighbours come by flocks,
    And here they will be merry.

Now kings and queens poor sheep-cotes have,
    And mate with everybody;
The honest now may play the knave,
    And wise men play the noddy.

---

[3] In allusion to the old Christmas money-box, made of earthenware, which required to be broken before the money could be obtained.

Some youths will now a mumming go,
Some others play at Rowland-ho,
And twenty other gambols mo,
   Because they will be merry.

Then wherefore in these merry days
   Should we, I pray, be duller?
No, let us sing some roundelays,
   To make our mirth the fuller.
And, whilst thus inspired we sing,
Let all the streets with echoes ring,
Woods and hills, and everything,
   Bear witness we are merry.

ALL YOU THAT IN THIS HOUSE BE HERE.

[AT the Restoration, Christmas Carols once more came into fashion. The following pleasing little composition is extracted from " New Carrols for this Merry Time of Christmas," 1661.]

ALL you that in this house be here,
    Remember Christ, that for us died;
And spend away with modest cheer
    In loving sort this Christmas tide.

And, whereas plenty God hath sent,
    Give frankly to your friends in love:
The bounteous mind is freely bent,
    And never will a niggard prove.

Our table spread within the hall,
    I know a banquet is at hand,
And friendly sort to welcome all
    That will unto their tacklings stand.

The maids are bonny girls, I see,
  Who have provided much good cheer,
Which, at my dame's commandment, be
  Now set upon the table here.

And I have here two knives in store,
  To lend to him that wanteth one;
Commend my wits, good lads, therefore,
  That come now hither having none.

For, if I should, no Christmas pie
  Would fall, I doubt, unto my share;
Wherefore, I will my manhood try,
  To fight a battle if I dare.

For pastry-crust, like castle walls,
  Stands braving me unto my face;
I am not well until it falls,
  And I made captain of the place.

The prunes, so lovely, look on me,
  I cannot choose but venture on:
The pie-meat spiced brave I see,
  The which I must not let alone.

Then, butler, fill me forth some beer,
    My song hath made me somewhat dry;
And so again, to this good cheer,
    I'll quickly fall, courageously.

And for my master I will pray,
    With all that of his household are,
Both old and young, that long we may
    Of God's good blessings have a share.

CHEER.

[THE last and best verse of a doggerel old Carol *For Saint John the Baptist*, shows the hospitality usually experienced by singers of Carols in the olden time. The composition dates from the West Country,—Devon or Cornwall.]

NOW kindly for my pretty song,
    Good butler, draw some beer;
    You know what duties do belong
To him that sings so clear.
Holly and ivy, and drink to drive ye,
    To the brown bowl of berry;
With apples and ale, and a Christmas tale,
    We'll make this household merry.

OLD CHRISTMAS RETURNED.

[NOTHING is known concerning the origin of the following old Carol. Evans includes it in his "Old Ballads," and from this source it is now immediately derived. It was written in all probability just after the Restoration, when the limits within which the festivities of the season had been confined by the over-zealous Puritans were overstepped, and something like a revival of the old hospitality began to show itself. The original is entitled " *Old Christmas Returned;* or, hospitality revived; being a looking-glass for rich misers, wherein they may see (if not blind) how much they are to blame for their penurious house-keeping; and likewise an encouragement to those noble-minded gentry, who lay out a great part of their estate in hospitality, relieving such persons as have need thereof :—

> Who feasts the poor, a true reward shall find,
> Or helps the old, the feeble, lame, and blind."]

ALL you that to feasting and mirth are inclined,
Come here is good news for to pleasure your mind,

Old Christmas is come for to keep open house,
He scorns to be guilty of starving a mouse!
Then come, boys, and welcome for diet the chief,
Plum-pudding, goose, capon, minced pies, and roast beef.

A long time together he hath been forgot,
They scarce could afford for to hang on the pot;
Such miserly sneaking in England hath been,
As by our forefathers ne'er used to be seen;
But now he's returned, you shall have in brief,
Plum-pudding, goose, capon, minced pies, and roast beef.

The times were ne'er good since old Christmas was fled,
And all hospitality hath been so dead,
No mirth at our festivals late did appear,
They would scarcely part with a cup of March beer;
But now you shall have, for the ease of your grief,
Plum-pudding, goose, capon, minced pies, and roast beef.

The butler and baker, they now may be glad,
The times they are mended, though they have been bad;

The brewer, he likewise may be of good cheer,
He shall have good trading for ale and strong beer;
All trades shall be jolly, and have, for relief,
Plum-pudding, goose, capon, minced pies, and roast
beef.

The holly and ivy about the walls wind,
And show that we ought to our neighbours be kind,
Inviting each other for pastime and sport,
And where we best fare, there we most do resort,
We fail not for victuals, and that of the chief,
Plum-pudding, goose, capon, minced pies, and roast
beef.

The cooks shall be busied, by day and by night,
In roasting and boiling, for taste and delight;
Their senses in liquor that's nappy they'll steep,
Though they be afforded to have little sleep;
They still are employed for to dress us, in brief,
Plum-pudding, goose, capon, minced pies, and roast
beef.

Although the cold weather doth hunger provoke,
'Tis a comfort to see how the chimneys do smoke;

Provision is making for beer, ale, and wine,
For all that are willing or ready to dine;
Then haste to the kitchen, for diet the chief—
Plum-pudding, goose, capon, minced pies, and roast beef.

All travellers, as they do pass on their way,
At gentlemen's halls are invited to stay,
Themselves to refresh, and their horses to rest,
Since that he must be Old Christmas's guest;
Nay, the poor shall not wait, but have, for relief,
Plum-pudding, goose, capon, minced pies, and roast beef.

Now Mock-beggar Hall it no more shall stand empty,
But all shall be furnished with freedom and plenty;
The hoarding old misers, who used to preserve
The gold in their coffers, and see the poor starve,
Must now spread their tables, and give them, in brief,
Plum-pudding, goose, capon, minced pies, and roast beef.

The court, and the city, and country are glad
Old Christmas is come to cheer up the sad;

Broad pieces and guineas about now shall fly,
And hundreds be losers by cogging a die,
Whilst others are feasting with diet the chief—
Plum-pudding, goose, capon, minced pies, and roast beef.

Those that have no coin at the cards for to play,
May sit by the fire and pass time away,
And drink of their moisture contented and free—
" My honest good fellow, come here is to thee! "
And when they are hungry, full to their relief,
Plum-pudding, goose, capon, minced pies, and roast beef.

Young gallants and ladies shall foot it along,
Each room in the house to the music shall throng,
Whilst jolly carouses about they shall pass,
And each country swain trip about with his lass;
Meantime goes the caterer to fetch in the chief—
Plum-pudding, goose, capon, minced pies, and roast beef.

The cooks and the scullion who toil in their frocks,
Their hopes do depend upon their Christmas-box;

There are very few that do live on the earth
But enjoy at this time either profit or mirth;
Yea, those that are charged to find all relief,
Plum-pudding, goose, capon, minced pies, and roast
    beef.

Then well may we welcome Old Christmas to town,
Who brings us good cheer and liquor so brown,
To pass the cold winter away with delight,
We feast it all day, and we frolic all night;
Both hunger and cold we keep out with relief,
Plum-pudding, goose, capon, minced pies, and roast
    beef.

Then let all curmudgeons, who dote on their wealth,
And value their treasure much more than their health,
Go hang themselves up, if they will be so kind,
Old Christmas with them but small welcome shall find:
They will not afford to themselves, without grief,
Plum-pudding, goose, capon, minced pies, and roast
    beef.

NOW THRICE WELCOME CHRISTMAS.

[THE old almanacks often gave a new Carol in praise of the festive season. The following is taken from "Poor Robin's Almanack," 1695.]

NOW thrice welcome Christmas,
    Which brings us good cheer,
    Minced pies and plum-porridge,
Good ale and strong beer;
With pig, goose, and capon,
    The best that can be:
So well doth the weather
    And our stomachs agree.

Observe how the chimneys
    Do smoke all about,
The cooks are providing
    For dinner, no doubt;

But those on whose tables
  No victuals appear,
O may they keep Lent
  All the rest of the year!

With holly and ivy
  So green and so gay,
We deck up our houses
  As fresh as the day,
With bays and rosemary,
  And laurel complete,
And every one now
  Is a king in conceit.

CHRISTMAS DAY APPROACHES NEAR.

[This Carol, also, is taken from "Poor Robin's Almanack," 1711. I have seen it entitled "A Hint to the Fanaticks."]

NOW Christmas Day approaches near,
   Trim up the house with holly,
And set abroach the strongest beer,
   For neighbours to be jolly.
Let fanatics old customs blame,
   Yet Christmas is a High day,
Though they will fast upon the same,
   And feast upon Good Friday.

Good works are popishly inclined,
   Say they that none will do,
Yet they for pride can money find,
   And keep a coach also.

Thus, that which should relieve the poor,
  And feast them at this tide,
Is spent upon a coach and four,
  To maintain foolish pride.

Yet some there are, although but few,
  In whom more goodness lurks,
Who, to the poor will pity show,
  And show their faith by works.
I wish, for one, that these were twain,
  And knaves away all swept,
That honest Christmas, once again,
  With feasting may be kept.

CHRISTMAS CUSTOMS.

[" POOR ROBIN'S Almanack" again contributes a Carol to our collection. The date is 1700. The lines breathe that delightful union of simple piety and honest mirth that marks an unsophisticated age.]

NOW that the time is come wherein
   Our Saviour Christ was born,
The larders full of beef and pork,
   And garners filled with corn;

As God hath plenty to thee sent,
   Take comfort of thy labours,
And let it never thee repent
   To feast thy needy neighbours.

Let fires in every chimney be,
   That people they may warm them;
Tables with dishes covered,
   Good victuals will not harm them.

With mutton, veal, beef, pig, and pork,
    Well furnish every board,
Plum-pudding, furmity, and what
    Thy stock will then afford.

No niggard of the liquor be,
    Let it go round thy table;
People may freely drink, but not
    So long as they are able.

Good customs they may be abused,
    Which makes rich men so slack us,
This feast is to relieve the poor,
    And not to drunken Bacchus.

Thus if thou doest, 't will credit raise thee,
God will thee bless, and neighbours praise thee.

CHRISTMAS IS A COMING.

[WE are indebted to a quaint little volume of popular superstition and folk-lore, entitled, "Round About our Coal-Fire," (1734,) for the following Carol, abounding in allusions to old Christmas customs and merry-makings. The mirth of those times appears to have been more boisterous, but was doubtless quite as harmless as that indulged in at the present prude period.]

YOU merry, merry souls,
 Christmas is a coming;
We shall have flowing bowls,
 Dancing, piping, drumming.

Delicate minced pies,
 To feast every virgin,
Capon and goose likewise,
 Brawn, and dish of sturgeon.

Then for your Christmas-box
   Sweet plum cakes and money,
Delicate Holland smocks,
   Kisses sweet as honey.

Hey for the Christmas ball,
   Where we shall be jolly;
Coupling short and tall,
   Kate, Dick, Ralph, and Molly.

Then to the hop we'll go,
   Where we'll jig and caper;
Dancers all a-row,
   Will shall pay the scraper.

Hodge shall dance with Prue,
   Keeping time with kisses;
We'll have a jovial crew
   Of sweet smirking misses.

THE WASSAILERS' CAROL.

[A RUDELY printed paper of Carols affords us the following little piece. As it does not bear any evidence of a distinguished origin, no attempt has been made to discover the author. Its allusions to customs gone by, however, and a certain quaint simplicity, which we may seek for in vain in the compositions of the educated, will, perhaps, be deemed sufficient apologies for its insertion. The date is apparently some time in the beginning of the last century, although the last verse but one may be observed in the little Carol entitled " God bless the master of this house," given at page 174, and which, Ritson says, is as old as the time of James I. Many of these broadside Carols, doubtless, contain scraps of still earlier compositions.]

HERE we come a wassailing
 Among the leaves so green,
Here we come a wandering
 So fair to be seen.

Chorus.

Love and joy come to you,
And to your wassail too,

And God send you a happy new year,
                A new year;
And God send you a happy new year.
Our wassail cup is made of the rosemary tree,
So is your beer of the best barley.

We are not the daily beggars,
   That beg from door to door,
But we are neighbours' children,
   Whom you have seen before.

Call up the butler of this house,
   Put on his golden ring,
Bid him bring up a glass of beer,
   The better that we may sing.

We have got a little purse
   Made of stretching leather skin,
We want a little of your money
   To line it well within.

Bring us out a table,
   And spread it with a cloth,
Bring us out a mouldy cheese,
   And some of your Christmas loaf.

God bless the master of this house,
    Likewise the mistress too;
And all the little children,
    That around the table go.

Good master and mistress,
    While you're sitting by the fire,
Pray think of us poor children,
    Who are wandering in the mire.

WASSAILERS' CAROL.

[BRAND says (1795) the subsequent Wassailers' Carol, on New Year's Eve, is still sung in Gloucestershire. The Wassailers bring with them a great bowl, dressed up with garlands and ribbons. Dobbin, Smiler, and Fillpail refer successively to the horse, mare, and cow.]

WASSAIL! Wassail! all over the town,
Our toast it is white, our ale it is brown;
Our bowl it is made of a maplin tree,
We be good fellows all—I drink to thee.

Here's to Dobbin, and to his right ear,
God send our master a happy New Year;
A happy New Year as e'er he did see—
With my Wassailing Bowl I drink to thee.

Here's to Smiler, and to her right eye,
God send our mistress a good Christmas pie;
As good Christmas pie as e'er I did see—
With my Wassailing Bowl I drink to thee.

Here's to Fillpail, and to her long tail,
God send our master us never may fail
Of a cup of good beer; I pray you draw near,
And our jolly Wassail it's then you shall hear.

Be here any maids? I suppose there be some—
Sure they'll not let young men stand on the cold stone;
Sing hey, O maids, come troll back the pin,
And the fairest maid in the house let us in.

Come, butler, come bring us a bowl of the best,
And I'll hope your soul in heaven will rest;
But if you do bring us a bowl of the small,
Then down may fall butler, and bowl, and all.

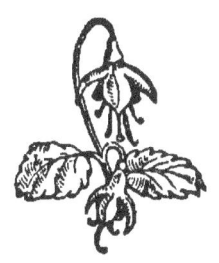

CAROL FOR THE POOR.

[ALTHOUGH a provincial broadsheet supplies the following, yet the Carol contains evidences of superior authorship. It was, probably, from the pen of one of the village poets of the last century, whose works, issued from a local press, and containing a list of the gentry and others well disposed to the author in the neighbourhood, are often to be noticed in collections of old books.]

E merry all, be merry all,
    With holly dress the festive hall,
    Prepare the song, the feast, the ball,
        To welcome merry Christmas.

And oh! remember, gentles gay,
To you who bask in fortune's ray,
The year is all a holiday,—
    The poor have only Christmas.

When you with velvets mantled o'er
Defy December's tempest's roar,
Oh, spare one garment from your store,
  To clothe the poor at Christmas.

When you the costly banquet deal
To guests, who never famine feel,
Oh, spare one morsel from your meal,
  To feed the poor at Christmas.

When gen'rous wine your care controls,
And gives new joy to happiest souls,
Oh, spare one goblet from your bowls,
  To cheer the poor at Christmas.

So shall each note of mirth appear
More sweet to heaven than praise or prayer,
And Angels, in their Carols there,
  Shall bless the poor at Christmas.

CHISWICK PRESS:—WHITTINGHAM AND WILKINS,
TOOKS COURT, CHANCERY LANE.

New Books Published by
JOHN CAMDEN HOTTEN,
151 PICCADILLY, LONDON, W.

Nearly ready, in small 4to, half morocco, very neat,

An hitherto unknown Poem, written by John Bunyan, whilst confined in Bedford Jail, for the support of his Family, entitled,

PROFITABLE MEDITATIONS, FITTED TO MAN'S DIFFERENT CONDITION; in a Conference between Christ and a Sinner. By JOHN BUNYAN, Servant to the Lord Jesus Christ. *London: Printed for Francis Smith at the Sign of the Elephant and Castle, without Temple Bar,* 1661.

This very interesting literary memorial of the Author of the celebrated "Pilgrim's Progress," has been choicely reprinted by Whittingham, from the only known copy lately discovered by the publisher. It is edited, with an Introduction, by George Offor, Esq. The impression is limited.

Now ready, price 5s.; by post, on roller, 5s. 4d.

MAGNA CHARTA. An Exact Facsimile of the Original Document, preserved in the British Museum, very carefully drawn, and printed on fine plate paper, nearly three feet long by two feet wide, with the ARMS AND SEALS OF THE BARONS ELABORATELY EMBLAZONED IN GOLD AND COLOURS. A.D. 1215.

COPIED BY EXPRESS PERMISSION, and the only *correct* drawing of the Great Charter *ever taken*. This important memorial of the liberties and rights of Englishmen is admirably adapted for framing, and would hang with propriety from the walls of every house in the country. As a guarantee to the purchaser that the facsimile is exact, the publisher need only state that Sir Frederick Madden has permitted copies to hang for public inspection upon the walls of the Manuscript Department in the British Museum. It was executed by Mr. Harrison, under whose auspices the splendid works on the Knights of the Garter was produced some years ago.

Preparing for publication, beautifully printed, post 8vo, half morocco.

GARLAND OF PEPYSIAN BALLADS, HISTORICAL, ROMANTIC, AND HUMOROUS, some illustrating Shakespeare, edited by EDWARD F. RIMBAULT, Esq., LL.D.

It is well known that the unfortunate regulation imposed by Pepys, the celebrated diarist, that his Manuscripts and Books should never be examined save in the presence of a Fellow of the College at Cambridge where they are preserved, has hitherto alone prevented the collecting and publishing some of the more interesting of these world-renowned Ballads and Songs. The difficulty, however, has been surmounted by Dr. Rimbault, aided by the authorities of Magdalene College; and the lovers of our charming old popular poetry will be glad to know that a *Garland* of these Balladian ditties is in course of publication. The work will be preceded by an Introduction on Ballad Lore, Ballad Writers, and Ballad Printers, giving some new and interesting particulars gathered from "old bookes," and other sources, hitherto unexplored. The publisher would state that the work will be beautifully printed by Whittingham, and that it will be adorned by a curious woodcut facsimile frontispiece.

New Books.

Nearly ready, beautifully printed, on fine paper, fcap. 8vo. pp. 350, price, 5s.

THE HISTORY OF PLAYING CARDS, AND THE VARIOUS GAMES connected with them, from the Earliest Ages; with some Account of Card Conjuring, and Old-Fashioned Tricks. *Illustrated with sixty curious woodcuts on tinted paper.*

This most amusing work, introducing the reader to a curious chapter of our social history, gives an interesting account, replete with anecdotes, of the most popular and widely known pastime which has ever been invented by man for his amusement.

Preparing for publication, fcap. 8vo, beautifully printed.

OLD ENGLISH BALLADS, relating to New England, the Plantations, and other Parts of North America; with Ancient Poetical Squibs on the Puritans and the Quakers who emigrated there; now first collected from the original excessively rare Broadsides sold in the streets at the time, and edited with Explanatory Notes. *Illustrated with facsimiles of the very singular woodcuts which adorn the original Songs and Ballads.*

Fcap. 8vo., cloth, price, 3s. 6d., beautifully printed.

GOG AND MAGOG; OR, THE HISTORY OF THE GUILDHALL GIANTS. With some Account of the Giants which Guard English and Continental Cities. By F. W. FAIRHOLT, F.S.A. *With illustrations on wood by the author, coloured and plain.*

** A most humorous and interesting little volume.

Second Edition, beautifully printed, 12mo, cloth, 3s. 6d.

THE CHOICEST HUMOROUS POETRY OF THE AGE.

THE BIGLOW PAPERS. By James Russell Lowell. *With coloured illustrations by George Cruikshank.*

*** This Edition has been Edited with additional Notes explanatory of the persons and subjects mentioned therein, and is the only one adapted to the English reader.

"The rhymes are as startling and felicitous as any in 'Hudibras.' 'Sam Slick' is a mere pretender in comparison."
— *Blackwood's Magazine.*

There is an edition of this work extant, hastily got up after my own was announced, edited by Mr. Hughes, the author of *Tom Brown's School Days.* It gives an introduction, long and occasionally amusing, but of not the least value in explaining to the *English* reader the peculiarities of the work. The *Globe* pointed out this sad defect in reviewing the present edition:—" The copy beside us," remarks the writer, " is apparently edited and published by Mr. Hotten, who gives a preface—which has the rare merit of explaining exactly what the ordinary English reader requires to know of satirical political poems, written in the Yankee dialect, touching the Mexican war, and the extension of the slave states—and of attempting to explain nothing else."—*Globe.*

LONDON: JOHN CAMDEN HOTTEN, PICCADILLY.

www.ingramcontent.com/pod-product-compliance
Lightning Source LLC
Chambersburg PA
CBHW021839230426
43669CB00008B/1017